The Positive Psychology Workbook Series

Invitation to Positive Psychology:
Research and Tools for the Professional
Robert Biswas-Diener

Positive Identities:
Narrative Practices and Positive Psychology
Margarita Tarragona

Positive Motivation
Kennon Sheldon

Positively Happy:
Routes to Sustainable Happiness
Sonja Lyubomirsky & Jaime Kurtz

Positive Acorn

http://www.positiveacorn.com

Table of Contents

Published 26 February 2014 (Revised 2019)
San Bernardino, CA
ISBN 9781483918723

Week 1   Your Stories, Your Selves

"Do you ever feel you have become the worst version of yourself?" Joe Fox asks Kathleen Kelly in You've Got Mail (Ephron, 1998). It is one of my favorite movies.[1] The two main characters, business rivals who dislike each other, start an email correspondence without knowing each other's actual identities. Through their exchanges they get to know each other in a different way. (If you have seen the picture, you know that they fall in love in the end. I am a sucker for romantic comedies.)

". . . become the worst version of yourself." The phrase struck me and has stayed with me for years because, as a therapist and coach, I like the fluidity of the term "becoming," the idea of "versions," and the possibility of having different versions of ourselves. I love classical music and I know that Beethoven's 9th Symphony can sound very different depending on the orchestra that plays it and who is conducting it. Beethoven's 9th is always Beethoven's 9th.   It has certain notes and a specific instrumentation. It will never sound like Mozart's Little Night Music or like The Beatle's "I Wanna Hold your Hand." But, still, we cannot say that Beethoven's 9th sounds only one way. There is ample room for a variety of nuances, tempos, moods and expressions that allow the piece to be played quite differently.

Something similar can be said about people. The notion of "versions" fits very well with contemporary thinking about identity in psychology: that there is not just one self, but versions of ourselves. We can choose to embody, bring forth, or perform different ways of being, different versions of "who we are." This sense of possibility is very useful in processes of growth and transformation, like the one you are embarking on now.

This workbook is an invitation to explore different versions of yourself and to choose which ones are closer to your dreams, values and commitments, to the kinds of relation-ships you want to have, and to your preferred way of being. It is inspired by two rich sources of knowledge: positive psychology and narrative practice. I will tell you a little about each of these.

_____

Positive Psychology

Positive psychology is the scientific study of well-being, of the factors that contribute to people and communities functioning at their best, of what helps us lead happier and more meaningful lives. Researchers in positive psychology are studying fascinating topics, such as positive emotions, optimism, gratitude, creativity, humor, goal setting and accomplishment, spirituality, optimal or "flow" experiences, values and character strengths, and transcendence and resilience, to name just a few. It is easy to see why Christopher Peterson, one of the most outstanding researchers in the field, likes to define positive psychology as the study of "what makes life worth living" (Peterson, 2006).

Narrative and Collaborative Practices

"Narrative" and "collaborative" approaches are important influences my work with people as a coach, therapist and consultant and they focus on particular ways of having conversations and dialogues. They are the philosophical stance that guides my relationships with clients and the way I approach this book, too, because even if we are not speaking with each other face to face, we will interact through this workbook.

"Narrative practices" are based on the idea that our "stories" play a very important role in our lives. One of the central premises of narrative practice is that the ways in which we narrate our experiences have a big impact on how we feel and think, on how we see ourselves and our relationships, and how we relate with other people.

"Collaborative"[2] work is based on the premise that we give meaning to our world though language, and that conversation and dialogue can generate meaning and possibilities.

---

[2] I will also use the term "dialogical" as synonymous with collaborative, since both dialogue and collaboration are the bases of this approach.

Both narrative and collaborative approaches propose that the way in which we think and talk about our experiences can either make problems bigger or help us contemplate new possibilities. When have certain kinds of conversations, we can build solutions and develop new stories and identities (Tarragona, 2008).

In this book we will bring together two kinds of experts and two sets of knowledge. On one hand, I will share with you what some of the brightest researchers in positive psychology have discovered about well-being, happiness, and human flourishing. Their scientific findings are generally expressed in terms of statistical averages and probabilities. Many of their studies are based on very large samples of people, which means that their results are likely applicable to most of us.

Statistical trends can tell us a lot about what is likely in large populations, but they do not predict particulars about a specific individual. So, for example, if research shows that, in general, people who are married tend to be happier, this does not mean that if you are not married you are not happy. I invite you to be open and curious about all the research data and consider if and how it can be relevant for your own life.

And here is the other expertise in the workbook: you, the expert in your own life[3]. Through different exercises and opportunities for reflection, I would like you to access your own knowledge about what contributes to your well-being and your preferred ways of being.

One feature of collaborative and narrative work is that these approaches emphasize and inquire about what works well in people's lives. They give priority to what clients consider important and valuable.

Narrative practitioners explore the clients' purposes, values, dreams, hopes, and commitments as well as the times they have influence over the problems that trouble them (White, 2004). In collaborative consultation, seeing language as fluid and potentially transforming allows us to have a hopeful attitude in our work and "to appreciate that human beings are resilient, that each person has contributions and potentials, and

---

[3] One of the mottos of collaborative work is "the client is the expert", meaning that nobody knows more about your own life than you do.

that each person's values wind and strive toward healthier successful lives and relationships" (Harlene Anderson 2006, p. 11). Anderson (2006) mentions the similarity between the hopefulness of collaborative therapies and positive psychology, which is more promising than deficit-based psychology.

Another point of convergence has to do with personal agency. Our capacity to choose and to act willfully is central to positive psychology. In narrative practice, White and Epston (1989) often use the metaphor of "being in the driver's seat of one's life."

Pushed by the Past; Pulled by the Future

Some influential views in psychology have proposed that people usually act in response to unconscious impulses and are driven by forces beyond their control. These perspectives believe that childhood experiences are strong determinants of adult behavior. Dr. Martin Seligman (2007) argues that there is no strong evidence to support this view and that we are not prisoners of the past, but that we can make choices. Positive psychology is inspired by a psychological and philosophical tradition that focuses on people's voli- tion and purposes as motivators for their behavior. Seligman actually defines positive psychology as the study of what people choose freely, what we choose for its own sake (2011).

In his closing address at the 1st Positive Psychology World Congress, Dr. Seligman said, "The problem with psychology in the twentieth century was to think that people are pushed by the past, instead of thinking that they are pulled by the future" (2009).

Research in positive psychology has produced a large body of scientific information about the factors that contribute to our well-being and tools to help us flourish. Narrative and collaborative practices have developed useful ways to have conversations, with ourselves and with others, to explore our values, skills, commitments and dreams, in order to bring us closer to how we prefer to be. I believe that, together, these two fields can help you be pulled by your future and become "the best versions of yourself."

Suggestions on How to Use this Workbook

Have you heard the saying, "Tell me and I forget. Teach me and I remember. Involve me and I learn?"[4] My intention is for you to be as involved as possible. I hope that you will be actively participating in a dialogue with this workbook, with yourself and with other people. As you do this, I hope that you will discover, recover, and strengthen significant stories and new possibilities for yourself. This workbook invites you to write and to have conversations every week. While part of it is already written and printed, the most important part is still blank. You will be the co-author of your own personalized version of this workbook by completing the exercises, which are designed to help you "bring home" and experience firsthand the ideas it presents.

Writing has important benefits for us. Dr. James Pennebaker, a psychologist from the University of Texas at Austin, has conducted many studies for over 30 years, which have shown how writing can help people overcome traumatic experiences, clarify their thoughts, acquire and retain new information more easily, solve problems, and even have better health and immune functions (Pennebaker J., 2004, 1997).

Dr. Laura King and her team of researchers from the University of Missouri have also studied the benefits of writing and have found that writing about their "best possible self" can help people feel more hopeful and be more engaged in their lives. She has also found that people who write about their goals are more likely to achieve them (Burton & King, 2009).

I hope that hearing about these research findings encourages you to write in your workbook. Don't worry about how you write, about your grammar, penmanship or spelling. This workbook is your own and nobody has to see it unless you want to share it. It is important that you feel free to enter into it your genuine thoughts and feelings.

Each chapter also has a "Conversation Exercise" that invites you to have a conversation with someone about one of the topics of the workbook. The intention of these is simply for you to engage in a meaningful conversation, to be guided by your curiosity about

---

[4] Attributed to Benjamin Franklin and also known as a Chinese proverb.

ideas and about the other person. Think of yourself as a journalist or researcher who is trying to understand as much as possible about your conversational partner's perspective. See each other as partners in a joint discovery. In my experience, 3 useful guide- lines for a productive conversation are: Don't judge, don't criticize, and don't offer advice. Just really pay attention and be interested in what the other person has to say.

As its name implies, a workbook is work. Like anything worth accomplishing, strengthening your positive identities will require effort and perseverance. The good news is that positive psychology and narrative-dialogical practices can help make this work fun and meaningful as you embark on this project.

Let's start with a simple exercise to warm up.

Exercise 1.1 Preferred Versions

Think of a song a song you like that has been performed by more than one singer or group. Also think of a movie that is a remake of an earlier film that you have also seen. List them and answer the following questions:

A. **Name of the song** _____
Version 1 sung/performed by Version 2 sung/performed by

_____

How are these two versions different?_____

_____

Which one do you prefer?_____

Why? What do you most appreciate about your preferred version?_____

_____

B. Name of the Movie (remake) _____
Who is in it or directs it?_____
Name of the original film_____

Who is in it or directs it?_____

How are these two versions different?_____

_____

Which one do you prefer?_____

_____

Why? What do you most appreciate about your preferred version?_____

_____

"What does this have to do with me?" you may ask. Obviously, you are much more complex than a song or a movie. But just as you took some time to think about why you prefer one rendition of a work over another, and you were able to decide which one you prefer and why, the exercises in this workbook will invite you to examine different versions of yourself and decide which ones are closer to what you prefer and value.

Psychologists used to think that a person's identity was basically formed in childhood and fine-tuned in adolescence and early adulthood, that this identity was more or less fixed, and that not much could be done to change that. Nowadays, psychology holds a more complex and, I believe, more hopeful view of identity.

There is convincing evidence that there are some things that we cannot change, features that may be genetically determined or established early in our lives. But there are also many aspects of us that can be modified or developed.

Martin Seligman, one of the founders of positive psychology, has written about what we can and what we cannot change (Seligman, 2007). He notes, for example, that it is very hard to change one's "set" weight range, or sexual orientation, while we can change our thought habits, such as pessimism, our fears, and a range of behaviors that can be problematic.

Sonja Lyubomirsky, one of the most noted researchers on happiness, has found that about half our happiness is determined by our genes, around 10% by our circumstances, and up to 40% by our choices and behaviors (Lyubomirsky, 2007). George Vaillant (Vaillant, 2002), who heads the most extensive longitudinal study of human development, has found that as we mature we are less influenced by our early experiences and much more affected by our choices, attitudes and actions.

Here is where the idea of different "versions" fits in. What we cannot change may be akin to the notes in a musical score. We may not be able to change if we are a Beethoven symphony or a Rolling Stones' song, but we have choices about the ways in which we can express and interpret that score, we can make decisions about how we "perform" ourselves.

Lives as Stories

The metaphors or analogies that we chose to think about ourselves can have different effects on our understandings and our actions. For example, the creators of narrative therapy, Michael White and David Epston (1990), explain that if we think that people and relationships are like complex machines (an analogy borrowed from the physical sciences), we will probably see their problems as malfunctions in the machinery and the solution would be to repair them, as a mechanic would. An example of this is when we say that anger was building up inside us like steam in a pressure cooker and that the steam has to be let out or the cooker will explode. Someone who is guided by this metaphor would probably encourage the person to "vent" and express that anger to release the growing pressure.

If we choose an analogy from medicine, we may understand an issue as a symptom, and a solution would be to have a good diagnosis and intervene to cure the underlying cause. An illustration of this kind of metaphor would be thinking that a child's bad behavior in school is really a symptom of the conflicts his parents are having in their marriage. A practitioner who is guided by this analogy would probably want to work with the parents marital issues because they are the "real cause" of the child's problem, and may not do much to change things in the classroom because his school behavior is "just" a symptom.

We use these kinds of analogies all the time, often without thinking about their implications. In your own life, what analogies do you tend to rely on when you are trying to understand yourself, a relationship or a difficulty? Do you find yourself trying to figure out what is broken and how it should be fixed? Or do you think of difficulties as superficial manifestations or symptoms of deeper issues that are not readily accessible? How helpful are these for you? Are there other metaphors that help you make sense of things?

White and Epston (1990) propose that it is useful to think of human problems as stories. If difficulties are seen as certain kinds of stories, solutions can be found in the authoring of different, alternative stories (Tarragona, 2008). This is what is called the "Narrative Metaphor" or "Text Analogy."

The Text Analogy

Narrative psychology is a perspective within cognitive psychology that studies how people create meaning. Narrative psychology emphasizes the importance of stories in our lives because human beings organize their life experiences as stories (Anderson, 1997; Bruner, 1990; Gergen, 1994; Polkinghorne, 1988). What is a story? A series of events that are linked together through time, which have developments and outcomes and, most importantly, these interconnected events have meaning for the person (Morgan, 2000).

Would you agree? When you think about your life, do you see it as a collection of disconnected experiences, or have you "connected the dots" so that it has a certain cohesion that makes sense to you?

We can think of our lives as texts, as if each life were a novel or a play. We know that life is not really just a collection of stories, but it is a metaphor that opens up possibilities for transformation, both when we are feeling stuck and when we are doing well and want to flourish even more.

Jerome Bruner (1987), a psychologist from New York University, has studied the importance of narratives in our lives and says that we *become* [5] the narratives that we

---

[5] My italics

construct to tell our lives. He and other scholars believe that our life narratives not only describe experiences, but actually have an impact on how we live. The stories we tell about our lives are not simply accounts of our experiences, they also generate experiences: how we feel, what we think, what possibilities and obstacles we see for ourselves. Jill Freedman and Gene Combs (2010) put it this way: "The same events can be storied in a variety of ways and these different ways will make a difference in how life is experienced."

It is important to note that we do not create our stories in a vacuum or out of the blue. Each culture offers certain story "templates" that make some ways of talking about our lives more likely than others.

Let's bring this idea closer to home. Please try this exercise to get a sense of how the same events can be storied in different ways:

Exercise 1. 2 A Documentary about a Day in Your Life

A. Think of three people whom know you well. (For example: my sister, my wife or partner, my friend, my mother, my ex-spouse …)

B. Write their names or initials.

Person 1_____, Person 2_____, Person 3 _____

C. Imagine that each one of them is given a special assignment. They will each receive a video recorder and they will follow you around, unobtrusively, for a day and record everything you do. Then each person will produce a 30 minute documentary about you.

- **What would Person 1's video about you look like? What would be the tone of the piece? Which of your activities would it feature? Which of your characteristics would be evident? What story would it tell about you?_____**

_____

_____

_____

_____

• **What would Person 2's video about you look like? What do you think would be the tone of the piece? Which of your activities would it feature? Which of your characteristics would be evident? What story would it tell about you?**_____

_____

_____

_____

_____

_____

• **What would Person 3's video about you look like? What do you think would be the tone of the piece? Which of your activities would it feature? Which of your characteristics would be more evident? What story would it tell about you?**_____

_____

_____

_____

_____

_____

• **Which of these would be a "truer" documentary about you? Do you like one more than the others? Why?**_____

_____

_____

_____

What are your thoughts about this exercise? Since the 3 people were filming you, everything they recorded actually happened. All three would be "true stories." Still, each of these people, or "authors," probably chose to highlight certain things about you. Just as each of them had to edit their film to 30 minutes, we all have to "edit" our everyday experiences. We can't possibly process every single thing we experience in a day, so we tend to highlight some events, and these are often the ones that "fit" with certain ideas or stories about ourselves.

Stories and Identity

Theorists like K. Gergen (1994) propose that we are constantly revising our stories throughout our lives and that we modify the meaning of events and relationships. Our personal narratives are dynamic and they take place in our relationships and conversations with other people. We are constantly "telling and retelling" our stories and each telling is influenced by interaction with other people who are listening, participating, or reacting to what we tell. From this perspective, our identity is not set in stone; it is fluid. I like the way Harlene Anderson puts it when she says that the self "is an on-go-
ing autobiography; or, to be more exact, it is a self-other multifaceted biography that we constantly pen and edit (1997, p. 216)."

If you adopt this view, if you think about yourself as "an ongoing autobiography" or a multifaceted biography that you are constantly writing with the help of others, who would be your most important co-authors? Who are the people with whom you have relationships and conversations that have a significant impact on how you see yourself? As you continue to work on the following chapters, you may want to have some of these people present in your mind as you explore more about your preferred identities.

Exploring your Preferred Identities

The notion of "preferred identities" refers to the idea that there is more than one definition of you and that you may favor certain ways of being, which are guided by your values, hopes and commitments. It also means that you have some choice about the kind of person that you want to be. In this section you will do some exercises to explore your preferred identities. You will learn about the concepts of dominant stories and alternative stories and do some fun activities about dominant stories that may be affecting your life and your sense of who you are.

Let me introduce you to Laura, a busy professional and mother who felt that she was a very disorganized woman. Laura's office at home was full of papers everywhere--unpaid bills, copies of journal articles, folders, some old magazines. Every horizontal surface seemed to be covered in paper. Sometimes she was late paying her credit card bills because she could not find them. She needed an article by a certain author, but it was probably buried under tens of others and she could not retrieve it in time to teach her class. There were piles of CDs outside their boxes. She tried hard, she bought every book that she saw about clutter and how to get rid of it, but the books about organization became part of the clutter themselves!

Laura felt like giving up, maybe she was just disorganized by nature. But being disorganized made her feel very bad about herself as a professional, as a wife and as a mother. After all, she thought, children learn what they live. She felt that she was not being a good role model to them. If you walked into her office in her home you too would reach the same conclusion. Laura was a disorganized person if there was ever one.

But, if you knew Laura a little better, you might notice some things that did not fit well with the description of her as disorganized. Her office at work, for example, was immaculate. Everything was in its place. Books were perfectly organized; her professional magazines were kept in special cabinets and all of her documents were filed—including her professional bills and credit card statements. The magazines in the waiting room were neatly ordered. When people walked into her office, they often commented what a serene and peaceful environment it was.

Even more surprising, a few years ago Laura was the organizer of a large international conference. She had to keep track of all the arrangements. Two hundred people participated, and everything went smoothly. The conference was a great success. Hmmm, for a disorganized person, this is an intriguing contrast. Maybe there was more to her than disorganization…

In the following section we will see how sometimes we hold certain ideas about ourselves that may be constricting, and that it may be worth expanding our identities so they fit better with how we prefer to think of ourselves and be seen by others.

The word "identity" comes from the Latin term for "sameness." When we think of ourselves, we generally assume that we are one way, always the same. We tend to think and speak of our identity as a set of characteristics that make up one solid person. This helps us feel a sense of individuality and coherence. But sometimes that one way of being can become restrictive, especially if we are going through a rough time, are facing difficulties, or feeling stuck. Sometimes we feel that the way we describe ourselves, or how other people see us, is out of synch with our values, commitments, and the hopes that we have for our lives. If you feel that "there is more to me than this," it may be a good idea to expand the definition of who you are, to explore your preferred identities.

Exercise 1.3 Your Identity Scrapbook

Imagine that you have a scrapbook filled with pictures and mementos of your life, from your early childhood until today. Go through it in your imagination, and pick two snapshots that show you behaving in ways that you like. They can be moments in which you felt great pleasure or joy, times when you were very involved in something that brought you a sense of satisfaction, pictures that show an important relationship, or images that reflect an event that was particularly meaningful to you.

Please describe each of these two pictures or mementos as vividly as possible. Try to recreate the moment and live it again. Include examples of where you were, with whom, what you were doing, how you felt and any sensations that you can recall, such as sounds, smells, and colors.

1._____

_____

_____

_____

_____

2. _____

_____

_____

_____

_____

_____

Reflection

What was this exercise like for you? Would you say that remembering or identifying these different moments of your life put you in touch with different facets of yourself? Could you see some glimpses of how you prefer to be? What strikes you most about this exercise? _____

_____

_____

_____

_____

_____

Identity and Personal Agency

Many psychologists (Bruner, 1990, Bandura, 2006) think that our identity is connected to our sense of personal agency. That is, people are not just products of their circumstances or passive receptors of forces. They also make decisions, act intentionally, and can have an impact on many of the developments in their lives. Narrative practitioners also stress how we are agents in our lives and that our decisions and intentions are guided by our values, beliefs, and commitments (White, 2007). When we speak of "pre ferred identities" we usually refer to the ideas about ourselves that are congruent with what we believe and value.

Let's take some of the pictures that you chose from your imaginary scrapbook and look at them from this perspective.

Exercise 1.4 More on Your Identity Scrapbook: Values, Beliefs and Commitments

Please go back to the two pictures you selected from your scrapbook.

Selected Snapshot #1

What would you call this image or scene?_____

_____

Why did you choose it?_____

_____

What do you think it says about you in that moment?

_____

_____

Does it reflect something that you valued at the time or value now?

_____

_____

Does it show any commitment or belief that was (or is) important to you?

_____

_____

Who supported you in being that way? What relationship allowed you to be a good version of yourself then? _____

Selected Snapshot #2

What would you call this image or scene?_____

_____

Why did you choose it?_____

_____

What do you think it says about you in that moment?

_____

_____

Does it reflect something that you valued at the time or value now?

_____

_____

Does it show any commitment or belief that was (or is) important to you?

_____

_____

Who supported you in being that way? What relationship allowed you to be a good version of yourself then?_____

_____

Dominant and Alternative Stories

At the beginning of this chapter we spoke of how sometimes we feel constrained because we and/or other people may have reached certain conclusions about who we are. If these definitions or conclusions are too narrow, they do not include enough angles or nuances of our experience. In narrative lingo we call these "dominant stories."

What is a dominant story? Remember we said that stories are series of events that are linked through time in a meaningful way. A dominant story links a series of experiences in someone's life and connects them in a way that makes sense, but that leaves out other events or experiences that are also important for the person.

Here is an example:

John wakes up and almost panics when he realizes that his alarm clock did not go off. "Agh! I forgot to program it," he says, still half asleep. He rushes through breakfast and on his way to work he notices that his car is running on empty. "Oh, I was supposed to fill it up last night," he remembers. He gets to his office ten minutes late, and his co-worker tells him, "John, the manager wants to see you."

"Oh! The report!" John thinks, as he drags his feet into the meeting room to speak with his boss. The manager is upset because John's sales report was not very good, and he asks John to re-write parts of it. As soon as he comes back to his office and gets to his desk John starts to answer calls, but he is already falling behind with his sales goal for the day.

What are you thinking? Are you beginning to form an idea about the kind of person John is? A distracted man maybe, or perhaps someone who is hopelessly disorganized? Events seem to point in these directions.

Here is a graphic depiction of John's day, with each dot representing on event or experience:

John's Dominant Story

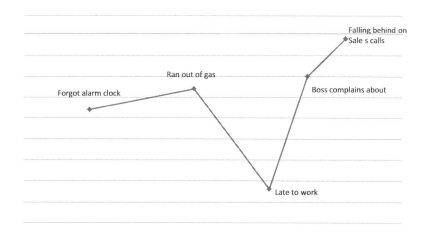

We can connect the following dots in the graph of John's day:

- Forgot to program alarm clock
- Ran out of gas
- Late to work
- Scolded by boss
- Late with sales calls

These connected events may give us the basis for a story about John. What kind of story comes to your mind? I think of things like incompetence, distraction, perhaps irresponsibility.

If instances like these happen frequently and they are what John and other people notice the most in his life, chances are he may think of himself as incompetent and this can become a dominant story that shapes his identity.

All of these events happened, but we did not mention that right after John woke up his two children stormed playfully into their parents' bedroom, followed by the dog. The children tickled and kissed John until they were all laughing hysterically. He took ten minutes to fix waffles for his children's breakfast. His wife Mary hugged him good-bye and wished him a good day as she handed him a homemade lunch. When he noticed that his car was running out of gas, his neighbor, who was also driving to work, stopped to ask him if he needed help. His neighbor reminded him about the many favors John had done for him over the years. After he had met with his boss at work, Julia from HR came looking for him. She asked him if he could organize the company's New Year's party since he had done such a good job last year. After that, Charlie, from the sales team, asked him if they could have lunch together, because he was going through some difficulties with his girlfriend and wanted to talk with John about what to do.

Here's a second graph portraying John's day:

An Alternative Story about John

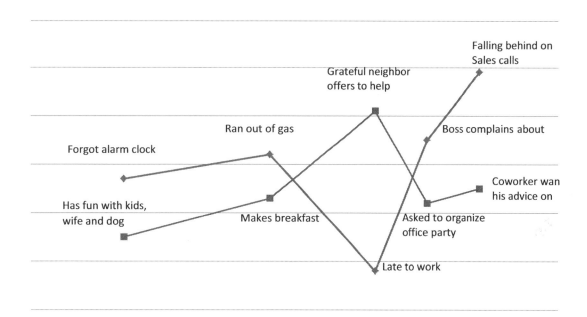

As you see, we can also connect the following dots or events in John's day:

- He wakes up surrounded by affection from children, wife and dog
- He takes time to make breakfast for his kids even though he is in a hurry
- His neighbor shows gratitude and appreciation for him because John has helped him in the past
- He did a good job organizing last year's office party and he is asked to do it again.
- Charlie values what John has to say about relationships and asks for his advice about his girlfriend.

Reflection

What ideas are you having about John now? Do you think that a different story is beginning to emerge when we also take into account the events you just connected? What are some of the words that come to your mind to describe John?

_____

_____

It is impossible to process and integrate every single experience that we have in our lives. We need to edit our stories, to select what we pay attention to and what is important. Imagine if everyone were to go through life with a yellow highlighter and highlight some of their experiences but not others. The experiences that we choose to highlight, and the dots that we connect become important stories in our lives. We need these important stories in order to understand our entire experience and make sense of who we are. When our focus is too narrow and we only include certain types of experiences and leave out others, we create a dominant story that may have detrimental effects for us.

The stories we tell ourselves about our experiences, and the stories about us that we share with others and hear from others, have an effect on how we see and understand ourselves. These stories have an impact on our identity.

Exercise 1.5 Dominant Stories about You

Dominant stories are often stated as a generalization about a person. For example: "She isn't any fun," or "He has no sense of humor," or "She is controlling and retentive."

A.   Take a minute to think of a time in your life when either you or someone close to you developed a "dominant story" about you that made you uncomfortable. For example, "She is always nervous;" "She's beautiful, but not the smart one;" "He is a poor leader;" "He has lots of emotional baggage;" "He can't focus." Write down a name for one of these dominant stories that you or other people have used to describe you.

1. A dominant story about me (or I have often been described as)

_____

_____

2. What have been the effects of this dominant story for you?

a. Has it affected the way you behave?

_____

b. Has it had an effect on any of your relationships?

_____

c. Has it had an effect on how you see yourself?

_____

d. Has it had an effect on your plans and dreams for the future?

_____

e. How do you evaluate these effects? Are they positive or negative for you?

_____

f. Does this dominant story fit with your values, commitments and hopes for the future? How so?

_____

_____

B.   What are some of the events or experiences that may have been "evidence" for this dominant story about you?

_____

_____

_____

_____

_____

3. Can you identify other events that do not fit with the dominant story, experiences that contradict it or are simply different from it? Write them down:

_____

_____

_____

_____

_____

_____

_____

_____

_____

_____

_____

4 . What would you call the alternative story that is emerging when you explore what is outside of the dominant story?

_____

_____

5. What effects do these glimpses of an alternative story have for you? What do they make you think and feel? Do they capture your imagination? How?

_____

_____

_____

6. How would this alternative story fit with what you believe and value? How does it affect your goals for the future?

_____

_____

_____

Chances are that the dominant story seems much clearer to you than the alternative one (It is, after all, dominant). This makes sense because the dominant story has had more attention and has been circulated and strengthened over time in your conversations and relationships. We could say it is a better developed story. Narrative practitioners say that we need to "thicken the plot" of alternative stories. To do so, we need evidence from our own experience.

Let's imagine a young woman, Anne, who has lived for a long time with a dominant story of shyness. She thinks of herself as shy. Ever since she was a child her family has called her "the shy one." She is very sensitized to noting the many times she behaves shyly at school. If a friend were to tell her, "Anne, you don't have to be shy," this encouragement would probably not have much of an impact on her. But if instead of trying to convince her, we could carefully explore with Anne the times when she has not acted shyly. Maybe if she looked at her life carefully, she would find instances in which she was outgoing, talkative, or outspoken. She could discover that finding first-hand evidence of non-shyness is helpful if she wanted to start leading a more outgoing life.

One of my favorite descriptions of narrative work is offered by Mary Sykes Wylie (1994). She says that finding clues for alternative stories is like panning for gold. Have you ever seen movies about the gold rush in California in the 19th century? People who wanted to find gold would spend hours and days dipping large sifters into rivers. The sifter would come out full of rocks and pebbles. People had to sift and sift through the rocks until, once in a while, they found a gold nugget. The gold nuggets for our identities are the times when we behaved differently from what our dominant story would tell us. They are the evidence of different possible stories about who we are.

Exercise 1.6 Panning for Gold

This is an exercise to do throughout the week. It will require you to hone your observation skills. Identify a dominant story about yourself that produces effects that you do not like. Be extra aware this week of any events, behaviors, or experiences in your life that do not fit with this dominant story. For example, Anne would need to pay attention to the events in her life where she did not behave shyly--the times when she may have been assertive, gregarious, or brave.

Please list a dominant story that does not fit with your preferred identity. For exam ple "I am a disorganized person", or "she has no patience", or "he is not reliable".

_____

List the clues for possible alternative stories (for example, times when you have been organized, patient or reliable).

_____   _____

_____   _____

_____   _____

Conversation Exercise Week 1:

> *Please get together with a friend or conversational partner. Talk about the idea of different versions of ourselves and preferred identities. Share your reactions and questions.*

Thank you for doing these exercises during Week 1. I hope you identified some dominant stories that may not reflect your preferred versions of yourself, and that you also found evidence for alternative stories that are more in line with how you like to be. I encourage you to keep exploring these alternative stories that will help you develop a "thick description" of yourself.

Readings for Week 1

Seligman, M.E.P. (2002). Authentic Happiness. New York: Free Press. Part 1.

Morgan, A. (2000) What is Narrative Therapy? Adelaide, Dulwich Centre Publications.

Additional Readings for Week 1

White, M. &. Epston, D. (1990). Narrative Means to Therapeutic Ends (1 ed.). New York: W. W. Norton & Company. Chap.1.

Freedman, J, & Combs, G. (1996). Narrative therapy: the social construction of preferred realities. New York: Norton. Chapter 3.

White, M. (2007). Maps of narrative practice. New York: W.W. Norton. Chapter 2

References

Anderson, H. (1997). Conversation, Language and Possibilities: A Postmodern Approach to Therapy. New York: Basic Books.

Bandura, A. (2006) Toward a Psychology of Human Agency, Perspectives on Psychological Science. Vol. 1(2) pp.164-180.

Bruner, J. S. (1990). Acts of meaning. Cambridge, Mass.: Harvard University Press.

Bruner, J. (1987 Spring). Life as Narrative. Social Research Vol. 54, No. 1.

Ephron, N. (Director). (1998). You've Got Mail [Motion Picture].

Freedman, J., & Combs, G. (1996). Narrative therapy: the social construction of preferred realities. New York: Norton

Freedman, J. &. (n.d.). Evanston Family Therapy Center. Retrieved September 19, 2010, from Characteristics of the Narrative World View: http://narrativetherapychicago.com/narrative worldview/narrative_worldview.htm

Gergen, K. (1997 (Original work published 1994). Realities and Relationships: Soundings in Social Construction. Cambridge: Harvard University Press. (Original work published 1994). Cambridge: Harvard University Press.

Lyubomirsky, S. (2007). The How of Happiness: A Scientific Approach to Getting the Life You Want. New York: Penguin Press HC.

Morgan, A. (2000). What is Narrative Therapy? Adelaide: Dulwich Centre Publications.

Peterson, C. (2006). A Primer in Positive Psychology. New York: Oxford University Press.

Polkinghorne, D. E. (1988). (1988). Narrative Knowing and the Human Sciences (Suny Series in the Philosophy of the Social Sciences). Albany, New York: State University Of New York Press.

Rambo, A., Heath, A & Chenail, R. (1993) Practicing Therapy. New York, Norton Books.

Seligman, M. (2009). Closing Keynote address. Philadelphia, Pennsylvania: 1st Positive Psychology World Congress.

Seligman, M. (2007). What You Can Change . . . and What You Can't*: The Complete Guide to Successful Self-Improvement. New York: Vintage.

Tarragona, M. (2008). Postmodern/Post-Structuralist Therapies. In Lebow, 21st Century Psychotherapies. Hoboken, NJ: John Wiley & Sons.

Vaillant, G. (2002). Aging Well: Surprising Guideposts to a Happier Life from the Land mark Harvard Study of Adult Development. . Boston: Little, Brown and Company.

White, M. & Epston, D. (1990). Narrative Means to Therapeutic End

White, M. (2007). Maps of narrative practice. New York: W.W. Norton.

This chapter will ask you to consider a different way of thinking about the problems and obstacles you may be facing in life. It presents a bold idea: your problems are not necessarily a reflection of your identity. Problems are problems, and you are you. The exercises for this week will invite you think, speak and write about problems as entities that are separate from you and to observe the effects that taking this perspective has on you.

This week I will ask you to think of yourself as an agent in your own life and to look at some of your important decisions, commitments and hopes for your future. The exercises in this chapter require curiosity and an open mind. In my experience, people who do them often get a broader perspective on themselves and feel a renewed sense of possibilities. I am excited to share them with you and hope you are ready to give them a try.

Thickening the Plot

By now, you have probably noticed some clues or possible evidence of different stories about who you are. Think about an alternative story as a seedling. We need to nurture it so it can grow. A dominant story may seem like an oak; it may have been taking root for years. One way to strengthen these alternative stories is to explore them, to talk and write about them so we can see that these are not isolated or disconnected events. Instead, these events have something to do with our skills, our sets of knowledge, and our relationships with our values and commitments.

Another way to think about this is in terms of "thin descriptions" versus "thick descriptions" of ourselves. I am not talking about waist sizes. The terms "thin description" and "thick description" come from philosophy and anthropology and they refer to the difference between having a simplistic view of something or someone, in contrast to having a complex and multifaceted description of a person or phenomenon.

When I think about thin and thick descriptions, I often have the image of textiles. I think of the difference between cheese cloth, which is so thin that you can see through it, and a thick, colorful Mayan tapestry. The cheese cloth has only a few threads. You can easily see each of them and the weave is not very strong. The tapestry, in contrast, is made of many threads of different colors that are intricately interwoven and the resulting knit is thick, complex and strong. We can think of our stories and our identities in a similar way.

Our non-preferred dominant stories can be seen as thin descriptions, because they generally are one-dimensional. To develop better stories, or to weave more beautiful tapestries, we need to "thicken the plot" of our own life stories.

Exercise 2.1 Thickening the Plot about You

In the previous exercise you "panned for gold" and were like a detective searching for clues about experiences that do not fit with simplistic, thin descriptions of you. Please refer to your list of clues and choose one for this exercise. Now you will be asked to play the role of a journalist, inquiring in detail about this experience of yours. You can write down your answers or even ask a friend to interview you. Please answer the following questions.

Chose a clue from the list you made on page 25:_____

1. Tell me more about this experience or incident. Where were you? What were you doing? Who were you with? What did you do?

_____

_____

_____

2. Did you see the event as a step in a direction that you like? Why? If so, how did you prepare for this step?

_____

_____

3. Did anyone else notice what you did or said? Who noticed? Did this person comment on it, or say anything?

_____

_____

_____

4. What do you think that this event said about you to this person?

_____

_____

_____

5. If no one noticed, would you have liked someone to pay attention to this event? Why? What would they have had to see to realize that this was an important moment for you?

_____

_____

_____

6. What did this event tell you about yourself?

_____

_____

_____

7. Was it related to values or beliefs that are important to you? How?

_____

_____

_____

8. How does this event relate to some of your skills and knowledge?

_____

_____

_____

Problems Are Not Symptoms

Have you ever been in a situation in which you are facing a problem and you ask yourself, "What is wrong with me?!" "If my child does not want to go to school, maybe I am a bad mother." "If the guy I was dating decides he is not ready for a relationship, I must be doing something to attract men who are afraid of commitment." "If my salary is barely enough to pay for my children's tuition, maybe I am self-sabotaging because I secretly fear success."

We have learned to see difficulties as reflections of ourselves. It feels natural to think this way; we don't even question it. But some authors argue that this is a cultural product and that psychology has something to do with it.

Positive psychology and narrative practices are disciplines that come from different intellectual traditions, but they share a discomfort with the way psychology as a discipline evolved over the 20th century, and they propose new ways of thinking and practicing in today's world.

Positive psychology has been skeptical of the emphasis on deficit and pathology that has characterized most of the history of psychology. Martin Seligman and Mihaly Csikszentmihalyi, the "fathers" of positive psychology, have pointed out how, since World War II, psychology became mostly a science about healing. This was very important, but led to an unbalanced psychology in which little was known about what makes life worth living (Seligman & Csikszentmihalyi, 2000). Positive psychology studies people's optimal functioning and strives to discover and promote the factors that allow individuals and communities to live fully and flourish.

Kenneth Gergen is a psychologist who is part of a philosophical tradition called "social constructionism," which proposes that we construct or create our experiences of reality through language and our interactions with other people. Social constructionists believe that the words we use to describe our experiences do not only convey what we think and feel, but actually shape or construct how we think, feel and act based on these experiences.

Our Words and Our Worlds

In an article entitled "Therapeutic Professions and the Diffusion of Deficit (1990)," Gergen argues that therapists, despite their best intentions, have contributed to the creation of a culture in which more and more aspects of human experience are considered sick or pathological. Gergen shows how "the vocabulary of human deficit" has grown over a short period of time in human history. He points out that terms such as; "low self-esteem," "burned out," "addictive personality," and tons of similar words did not exist 100 years ago. He explains that these terms of mental deficit "discredit the individual, drawing attention to problems, shortcomings or incapacities (1991)" and that adopting these concepts can lead to "self-enfeeblement."

Try out this exercise to get a clearer sense about deficit language and its impact.

Exercise 2.2 Our Everyday Psychological Vocabulary

How often do you use these terms when you think or talk about yourself or other people in your life?

	Never	Sometimes	Often	Very Often
Low self-esteem				
Repressed				
Workaholic				
Codependent				
Anti-social personality				

	Never	Sometimes	Often	Very Often
Anorexic	_____	_____	_____	_____
Depressive	_____	_____	_____	_____
Obsessive	_____	_____	_____	_____
Anxious	_____	_____	_____	_____
Needy	_____	_____	_____	_____
Dysfunctional Family	_____	_____	_____	_____

There are no right or wrong answers. Some of these concepts may be quite useful for many people. Other times they may be limiting or problematic. The intent of the exercise is for us to reflect about the words we use and the effects that they have on us and others.

Reflection

Take a minute to think of an instance when one of the terms from the list above (or a similar one) has been used to describe you. What was it like? How did you feel? What did you think? Did it influence your subsequent actions somehow?

_____
_____
_____
_____
_____

One of the premises of narrative and dialogical work is that the words we use, individually and as a society, are very important. As the Norwegian psychiatrist Tom Andersen used to say, "language is not innocent," (1996) because what we understand depends a lot on what we hear and see, and what we hear and see depends on what we look for and listen to. The exercises you did last week had to do precisely with broadening what you choose to look for and listen to in your own life stories, so you can have richer description of who you are.

Internalizing and Externalizing Language

Michael White, one of the creators of narrative practice, said that many of the terms we use when we think about people refer to "internal states." Internal states include unconscious motives, instincts, drives, traits and dispositions (White, 2004). When we think along these lines, people's actions and expressions tend to be seen as surface manifestations of these internal states. The implication is that there are deep processes, to which we have little access, and that our behavior is a result of those invisible processes. A typical metaphor that illustrates this view is the "tip of the iceberg" image: what we see is just the little piece that is observable, but what is most important and bigger is below the surface.

An important consequence of adopting this "iceberg" framework is that problems are understood as manifestations of internal states. So, a person's difficulties are seen as symptoms or signs of a deeper deficiency or flaw. Difficulties are considered the visible signs of invisible flaws in our personalities. We think, "If I am having this problem, it means that I am_____." We see problems as a reflection of who we are, as part of our identity.

White (1990, 2004, 2007) and other authors, including Jerome Bruner (1990) have stressed that this "internal state" understanding of people is not the only available framework that we have. Different cultures and different times in history have adopted various ways of conceptualizing persons and problems. We have a choice about which frameworks to use. Narrative practitioners believe that an "internalizing" view of problems can often have negative consequences. They offer a different way of thinking and talking about human difficulties. But before telling you about it, I would like you to have a taste of this different language through the following exercise.

Exercise 2.3 Internalizing and Externalizing Conversations
[Adapted from Freedman and Combs, (1996)]

This exercise can be very interesting when it is done as an interview. If you can, find a friend or partner to ask you these questions out loud and take turns interviewing each other. Ask the person you are interviewing all of the questions in Parts 1 and 2, then switch roles.

If you prefer, you can interview yourself and write the answers down.

Part I.

Think of a personal characteristic of yours that you find difficult, something you are not too happy about, that may cause you troubles sometimes or that you might like to change about yourself.

Write down this characteristic as an adjective, "X." _____

(For example, our friend Laura from Chapter 2 would say that she is "disorganized."[6] Someone else may say he is "neurotic", another person may pick the adjective "anxious" to describe herself)

Please answer the following questions:

How did you become X?

_____
_____
_____
_____
_____

---

[6] Make sure it is an adjective. For example: lazy, disorganized, stressed, hyperactive, anxious.

Do you do things when you are X that you would not do if you were not X?

_____
_____
_____
_____
_____
_____

Are you currently experiencing any difficulties because you are X?

_____
_____
_____
_____
_____
_____

What is your self-image like when you are X?

_____
_____
_____
_____
_____
_____

Part II

Now take the same characteristic and turn it into a noun, "Y." [7]

_____

(For example, our friend Laura from Chapter 2 would transform the adjective "disorganized" into the noun "disorganization", the person who said he was "neurotic" would talk about "neurosis" and the one who said she was anxious would now choose the noun "anxiety")

What made you vulnerable to Y?

_____
_____
_____
_____
_____
_____
_____

Under what circumstances is it more likely that Y may take over the situation?

_____
_____
_____
_____
_____
_____
_____

---

[7] For example, if your adjective was "lazy", the noun would be "laziness"; if your adjective was "impatient", the noun would be "impatience", if you had chosen the adjective "insecure", the noun would be "insecurity"…

What effects does Y have on your life and your relationships with other people?

_____
_____
_____
_____
_____
_____
_____

Has Y led you to any difficulties you may be experimenting in the present?

_____
_____
_____
_____
_____
_____
_____

Have there been times in which Y might have taken over the situation but you did not let it happen?

_____
_____
_____
_____
_____
_____
_____

Reflection

Now please take a moment to reflect (or to talk with your partner) about what you just did.

What was it like to answer interviews A (adjective) and B (noun)?

What did interview A (adjective) make you think and feel?

How about interview B (noun)?

Did you notice any differences between talking about something as an adjective and as a noun?

If you did notice some differences, what were they?

Again, there are no right or wrong answers. But narrative practitioners often find that when we talk about problems as adjectives, we internalize them, we see them as reflections of our self, as essential characteristics that are hard to change because they are part of who we are. When we speak about a difficulty as a noun, we are externalizing it. We describe it as something separate from us: I am me, and the problem is the problem. This distinction often allows us to see problems from a different perspective and to feel that we have more options or space for maneuvering in our life. Does this make sense to you?

It is interesting how this externalizing perspective fits with some of the research findings about optimism in positive psychology. People with an optimistic outlook expect good things to happen. There are many studies that show that, in general, being optimistic is beneficial. When we are confident that we can achieve something, we act accordingly and persevere in our efforts even when circumstances are difficult (Carver & Scheier, 2005). Research shows that optimism helps people feel less distress in the face of adversity and to fare better under many stressful situations (Carver & Scheier, 2005). When something goes wrong, people who think optimistically often see it as a discrete event (For example, "I did not study enough for this exam; I will prepare better for the next test by going to math review every Thursday."), while pessimists tend to generalize it and see it as a reflection of themselves ("I am terrible at math; I will never pass this class."). We could say that pessimistic thought is "internalizing," while an optimistic style is "externalizing" when situations are difficult.

Personal Agency

We have seen how externalizing problems can be useful to separate our identity from the difficulties we may face in life. What are other narrative ideas that can help us move towards our preferred ways of being? Michael White (2004)[8] believed that it is very important to understand what makes people "tick" according to their intentions, purposes, values and commitments. A central feature of this psychology is the notion of personal agency: that people are active players in their own lives, they make decisions, can pursue what they find valuable and meaningful, and they behave intentionally. White (2004) suggests that when people want to change or want to be closer to their preferred selves, it is useful to inquire about their intentions, their values, commitments, hopes and dreams. [9]

In the final part of this chapter, we will look into the future, your future. Our goals, hopes and dreams can be as powerful, or more, than our history. Dr. George Vaillant (2002) has conducted one of the most important longitudinal research projects in the world, the Study of Adult Development at Harvard University. The research has followed a group of men for over 70 years, from their early twenties into their very old age. Among his subjects were some who were considered "at risk" because in their families of origin there was abuse, alcoholism and violence. Despite these difficult early experiences, many of these men took their life in their hands, made good decisions and demonstrated great resilience. Vaillant also found that one of the factors that allow adults to age well is to be oriented towards the future. Other studies of resilience have shown that having a positive view of oneself, self-confidence, and hope about the future

---

[8] Influenced by "folk psychology"

[9] This also fits with the ideas of William James, who spoke about the importance of free will and whose work has had a strong influence on Positive Psychology.

are all protective factors against developmental threats and foster resilience.

Dr. Laura King, a professor at the University of Missouri, has studied the importance that establishing goals has for our well-being. She has found that people who write down their goals are more likely to achieve them.[10] Dr. King has also studied the effects of writing about our "best possible future selves." She would ask participants in her research to visualize their best possible future in different areas of life and write about it for 20 minutes, four days in a row. Other participants had to write about a traumatic experience, because there was extensive evidence about the benefits of writing about trauma, including improved physical health. Dr. King found that people who wrote about their best possible selves showed a significant increase in their mood and happiness levels and that writing about best possible selves had health benefits comparable or greater than those brought about by writing about trauma, without the emotional discomfort of the latter (King, 2001).

Sonja Lyubomirsky, one of the most prominent researchers on happiness, did a similar study, but participants had to write once in the lab and then in their homes as frequently and as long as they chose (Lyubomirsky, 2007). She and her co-researcher, Ken Sheldon, also found an increase in the positive moods of people who wrote, and that those participants who felt that this exercise was a "good fit" for them and practiced consistently were the ones who benefitted the most from it.

 The exact instructions that Lyubomirsky and Sheldon used to explain what "best possible self" means were: "Imagine yourself in the future, after everything has gone as well as it possibly could. You have worked hard and succeeded at accomplishing all your life goals. Think of this as the realization of all your life dreams and your own best potentials (Lyubomirsky, 2007, p. 104)."

---

[10] Caroline Miller, MAPP, a coach who specializes in Positive Psychology and goal setting has written a wonderful website with many goal related resources: http://www.carolinemillercoaching.com

Exercise 2.4 Your Best Possible Self

Let's finish this week's exercises by following Drs. King and Lyubomirsky and writing about your best possible self.

_____

_____

_____

_____

_____

_____

_____

_____

_____

_____

_____

_____

_____

_____

_____

_____

_____

_____

_____

_____

_____

_____

_____

_____

_____

_____

Conversation Exercise Week 2:

> *Please get together with a friend or conversational partner. Talk about your ideas about "externalizing problems" (as when you spoke about a problem as an adjective and as a noun).*

Readings for Week 2:

Miller, C.A & Frisch, M.B. Creating your Best Life: The Ultimate Life List Guide.

Freedman, J., & Combs, G. (1996). Narrative therapy: the social construction of preferred realities. New York. Norton. Chap. 5.

References

Andersen, T. (1996). Language is not innocent. In F. W. Kaslow, Handbook of Relational Diagnosis and Dysfunctional Family Patterns (pp. 119-125). New York: John Wiley and Sons.

Bruner, J. S. (1990). Acts of meaning. Cambridge, Mass.: Harvard University Press.

Carver, C., & Scheier, M. (2005). Optimism. In C. Snyder, & S. Lopez, Handbook of Positive Psychology. New York: Oxford University Press.

Freedman, J., & Combs, G. (1996). Narrative therapy: the social construction of preferred realities. New York: Norton.

Gergen, K. J. (1990). Therapeutic Professions and the Diffusion of Deficit. The Journal of Mind and Behavior, Summer 1990, Vol. 11, No. 3, Pages 353-368.

King, L. A. (2001). The health benefits of writing about life goals. Personality and Social Psychology Bulletin, 798-807.

Lyubomirsky, S. (2007). The How of Happiness: A Scientific Approach to Getting the Life You Want. New York: Penguin Press HC.

Miller, C. A., & Frisch, M. B. (2009). Creating your best life: the ultimate life list guide. New York: Sterling.

Seligman, M. E. (2009). Closing Plenary 1st World Conference on Positive Psychology. Philadelphia, PA.

Seligman, M. E., & Csikszentmihalyi, M. (2000, Jan.). Positive Psychology An Introduction. American Psychologist, 5-14.

Vaillant, G. (2002). Aging Well: Surprising Guideposts to a Happier Life from the Landmark Harvard Study of Adult Development. Boston: Little, Brown and Company.

White, M. (2007). Maps of narrative practice. New York: W.W. Norton.

White, M. (2004). Narrative Practice and Exotic Lives: Resurrecting diversity in everyday life. Adelaide, South Australia: Dulwich Centre Publications.

Yates, J., & Masten, A. (2004). Fostering the future: Resilience theory and the practice of positive psychology. In P. A. Linley, & S. Joseph, Positive psychology in practice (pp. 521-539). Hoboken, NJ: John Wiley & Sons.

Week 3 PERMA and Positivity in your Life

This week we will talk about Dr. Martin Seligman's new theory of well-being and its five elements, summarized with the acronym PERMA. Through the remainder of the workbook, we'll discuss each of the five elements. In this chapter, we will focus especially on the "P" element—"Positive Emotions"—and the role that they play in your life. Through different exercises, I will invite you to reflect about different positive emotions and how you can cultivate them to increase your well-being.

A New Theory of Well-Being

Dr. Martin Seligman, one of the founders of Positive Psychology, has recently written a book called Flourish: A Visionary New Understanding of Happiness and Well-Being (2011). In it, he refines his previous ideas about happiness. He now prefers to think in terms of well-being, because happiness is usually associated almost exclusively with being cheerful and feeling good, and this is a simplification of what positive psychology
studies. Positive psychology, Seligman explains, is not just about feeling happy, its goal is to understand what we choose "for its own sake" (2011, loc.343).

We often choose things that make us feel good, but we also opt for choices that may be unpleasant but worthy for other reasons. For example, it is more pleasurable to go to the movies than to stay home and study for a final exam. But passing the exam may be tied to our goals and dreams for the future, or it may be part of a commitment we made to ourselves or to our family, so we stay glued to the seat and study instead of enjoying popcorn and a film.

Well-being, according to Seligman (2011) is a construct (not a concrete "thing," but a concept) that has several elements that can be measured. These elements are: positive emotion, engagement, meaning, positive relationships and accomplishment. The mnemonic device PERMA can help us remember what they are. Each of these elements is important and they can all be indicators of well-being.

Positive Emotions

Can you identify when you have felt very enthusiastic lately? How much awe have you experienced this week? When did you last feel truly grateful? What has brought you most joy today? These are the kinds of questions that Dr. Barbara Fredrickson has developed to help people explore their positive emotions and to research positivity.

Dr. Barbara Fredrickson is a psychologist and a professor at the University of North Carolina in Chapel Hill. She is one of the world's leading researchers in positive psychology and she specializes in the study of feelings, the physiology of emotions and well-being.

People intuitively classify their feelings as negative or positive. Even though they are all part of the range of human emotions (and arguably we need to experience and possibly accept them all), we know that we like to feel strong, alert, inspired or loving, and we generally prefer not to feel angry, sad, anxious or repulsed.

Psychologists have studied emotions for over a century, but until recently, they had concentrated only on the negative emotions, particularly depression, anger and anxiety. Barbara Fredrickson (2003) explains that there is a consensus among researchers about the role that negative emotions have played in our evolution as a species. Fear, anger and anxiety are like alarms that prepare us to respond in the face of danger. They are a central part of the famous "fight or flight reaction."

Imagine that one of our ancestors who lives in a Neolithic cave ventures outside and suddenly runs into a tiger. He has two choices: either fight the tiger or run as fast as he can. "Fight or flight." Even though we rarely face wild animals in our urban lives today, our bodies have not changed that much. Physiologically, we react in much the same way as our distant Neolithic relatives did.

Interestingly, as Fredrickson (2003) points out, these negative emotions have very clear physical signs, such as changes in blood pressure, sweating and body temperature. But pleasant emotions generally do not have clear physiological correlates. We know much less about positive emotions, and for years almost nobody studied them. Barbara Fredrickson wondered if positive emotions also may be useful in some way, and the results of her investigations have been surprising.

Dr. Fredrickson and her team have devised ingenious ways to evoke positive emotions in people who participate in their studies. For example, when people arrive to the lab, they show them a funny video or they give them a chocolate or a small gift and after that they are asked to answer some tests. Fredrickson discovered that when people feel positive emotions their short-term memory and concentration improve and they perform better on verbal tasks (2003, 2009). They are also more open to new information. Data show that positive emotions improve visual attention and verbal creativity, and that students do better in standardized tests if they feel positive emotions before taking the exams.

An experiment found that doctors who felt positive emotions before conducting a clinical examination on patients were less likely to reach a premature diagnosis and did a better job integrating the information of the clinical exploration. Studies with business people show that managers who experienced positive emotions are more careful and precise in their decision-making processes and more effective in their interpersonal relationships. Other studies in the workplace have demonstrated that people who come to a negotiation table feeling positive emotions get better results. Fredrickson has found that these kinds of effects are not exclusively American or Western, but common across different cultures, such as India and Japan (2009).

Based on her numerous studies on the relationship between positive affect and cognitive functioning, Fredrickson believes that positive emotions play a role in human evolution. They encourage us to explore our environment, to be open to information, to learn better, and to experiment, create and build. She has called her theory the "Broaden and Build" theory (Fredrickson, 2009).

Many studies show that positive emotions are good for people. In the long term, people who experience more positive emotions are more satisfied with their lives, have better relationships, better jobs and even live longer (Harker & Keltner, 2001; Danner, Snowdon & Friesen, 2001).

One could wonder which came first, the chicken or the egg. Are people feeling more positive emotions because they have better jobs or better marriages? Or do they have better lives because they feel more positive emotions? But the statistical techniques that have been used and the data from longitudinal studies (which follow the same group of people over time) allow us to see the direction of the relationship. Positive feelings actually predict success, satisfaction and longevity.

Dr. Fredrickson goes beyond positive emotions and talks about "Positivity" (2009), which also includes positive attitudes and thoughts. She has found that there are ten forms of positivity that are widely recognized and that people report most often. Can you discover what they are?

Exercise 3.1 Find 10 forms of Positivity

Hidden in this puzzle are the 10 forms of positivity. Find them and write them down.

Q	F	T	T	E	I	H	B	E	O	S	C
E	A	T	J	M	R	O	G	I	F	E	O
N	E	F	I	O	I	P	R	Q	W	R	D
E	O	H	A	I	Y	E	A	A	L	E	F
I	N	S	P	I	R	A	T	I	O	N	S
F	I	A	T	V	F	M	I	O	V	I	U
N	T	S	L	R	D	W	T	E	E	T	C
I	F	N	S	E	I	E	U	S	E	Y	R
R	C	U	D	E	Y	V	D	I	S	B	U
T	A	I	N	T	E	R	E	S	T	K	G
D	R	M	N	S	I	W	L	L	Y	E	S
P	P	G	L	D	A	E	H	G	S	C	C

_____   _____

_____   _____

_____   _____

_____   _____

_____   _____

Pst, pst... if this is too hard[11]

---

[11] (Answers: joy, gratitude, serenity, interest, hope, pride, fun, awe, inspiration, love)

Fredrickson talks about these forms of positivity: gratitude, serenity, interest, hope, pride, fun, inspiration, awe and love (2009). She describes them as follows:

Joy We feel joy when things go well, even better than expected, and do not require much effort. Joy makes you want to take everything in, to play, to get involved (Fredrickson 2009, p.40).

Gratitude happens when we appreciate something that we have received as a gift. It makes us want to give back, to do something good for someone. It is like a mixture of joy and appreciation. (2009, p.41)

Serenity is similar to joy in that it happens when we are safe and does not require an effort on our parts, but it is calmer than joy. According to Fredrickson, serenity makes us want to stop where we are and savor our experience (2009).

Interest is not as effortless; you want to explore what you are discovering. "You feel open and alive . . . Interest is what pulls you to explore, to assimilate new ideas and to learn more," says Fredrickson (2009. p.43).

Hope can exist when things are not going well or we are facing uncertainty. According to Fredrickson, what underlies hope is the belief that things can change for the better and there are possibilities. Hope keeps us from falling into desperation and motivates us to use our resources to turn things around. It inspires us to plan for a better future (2009, p.43).

Pride can be one of the Capital Sins, Fredrickson points out. But when it is specific and not excessive, it is clearly a positive emotion. We can feel proud when we are responsible for an accomplishment that required effort and skills and we want to share this with others. Pride can make you want to do more (2009).

Fun happens when something surprises us in a good way. When there are incongruities that are not dangerous, the situation is funny. Fun makes us want to laugh and share our enjoyment with other people (Fredrickson, 2009).

Inspiration is what we feel when we are in contact with excellence and this elevates us and makes us want to be better and reach the limits of our potential (Fredrickson, 2009).

<u>Awe</u> is similar to inspiration, but we feel it when we are overcome with beauty or excellence on a larger scale, such as in nature, for example. Fredrickson says that awe makes us feel part of something that is bigger than ourselves (2009, p.46).

<u>Love</u>, for Fredrickson, includes all of the other positive emotions: joy, gratitude, serenity, interest, hope, pride, fun, awe and inspiration. When we feel these emotions in the context of a relationship, we call it love (2009).

Exercise 3.2 Make a Wish

If the Positivity Fairy Godmother appeared today and said, "I will grant you one of the ten positive emotions, for you to feel as often as you want this week," which one would you choose? Please circle it:

Joy   Gratitude   Serenity   Interest   Hope   Pride   Fun   Awe   Inspiration   Love

The Fairy Godmother will be happy to grant you_____(chosen form of positivity), but since she is very curious, she will ask you some questions first:

Why did you choose_____(write the form of positivity you circled) at this time?

_____

_____

How familiar are you with_____?

_____

_____

Can you tell me about the most recent time you experienced_____?

_____

_____

_____

_____

What effect does_____have on your daily activities?

_____

_____

What effect does_____have on your relationships?

_____

_____

What effect does_____have on your plans for the future?

_____

_____

What effect does_____have on your sense of yourself?

_____

_____

If you could consult with an expert on_____, in order to feel more of this emotion in your life, who would that person be?_____

Do you have any ideas about the advice this person would give you?

_____

_____

Reflection

What are you thinking and feeling after answering these questions?

_____

_____

_____

Fredrickson summarizes the findings of over 300 research studies on positive emotions, in which thousands of people participated (2009). Data show that positivity has the following benefits in our lives:

- It builds psychological strengths such as optimism, resilience, acceptance, openness and sense of purpose.

- It builds good mental habits such as perseverance, concentration, mindfulness, savoring, and the ability to consider different ways to reach goals and solve problems.

- It builds social relationships because it is contagious; it strengthens bonds and makes us attractive.

- It builds physical health. Positivity correlates with having fewer physical symptoms, lower levels of stress hormones, and higher levels of growth hormones and progesterone (considered by some a relationship enhancing hormone). Positivity also increases our levels of dopamine, stimulates the immune system and lessens the inflammatory response caused by stress.

I imagine that after reading about all the benefits of positivity, you may be thinking about your own positive emotions. Let's look at one of them in more detail, in the following exercise.

Exercise 3.3 Do It Yourself

For this one, there is no Fairy Godmother. But imagine that you are given the freedom and resources to create the conditions that will guarantee that you will experience one of the ten forms of positivity today.

A. Choose one form of positivity (circle it).

Joy   Gratitude   Serenity   Interest   Hope   Pride   Fun   Awe Inspiration   Love

B. In order to make it almost certain that you will experience_____
(the positive emotion of your choice), answer these questions:

Where would you be?

_____

_____

What activities would you do?

_____

_____

With whom would you spend time?

_____

_____

Would you listen to music? If so, what would it be?

_____

_____

Would you read? If so, what would you read?

_____

_____

Would you watch any movies or TV shows?

_____

_____

What would be your "secret ingredient" for_____**? (chosen positive emotion)**

_____

Fredrickson and her collaborators have found that people who function optimally and flourish have something in common: they all experience more positivity than negativity in their everyday lives. We all have negative feelings. They are a normal part of life and, as we gave seen, they can play an important role in our well-being. The important thing is how often they occur in comparison to positive emotions. There is no exact ratio of positive and negative emotions that characterizes people who flourish, but Fredrickson's research has found that a preponderance of positive over negative emotions is very important for wellbeing.

Visit Dr. Fredrickson's website <u>http://positivityresonance.com/meditations.html</u> and try out one of her guided mediations. Try this at least twice a week.

Reflections

What was doing the guided mediation like for you?

Did you feel any effects of the meditation?

Any other comments?

Can we increase our levels of positivity? Fredrickson believes that we can. In her book, Positivity (2009), she offers many suggestions about how to do this, among them:

- Find positive meaning in our experiences
- Enjoy the good
- Be grateful and "count our blessings"
- Know what we are passionate about and do it.
- Dream about the future
- Use our strengths
- Connect with other people
- Connect with nature
- Open our minds
- Open our hearts

In the following chapters we will discuss several of these topics, such as connecting with others and knowing and using our strengths.

Flourishing

Like Seligman, Barbara Fredrickson is interested in "Human Flourishing." They use the term to refer to functioning optimally, with kindness, creativity and resilience. Flourishing goes beyond the absence of pathology; it includes the presence of positive functioning. According to Fredrickson, some people do not flourish, but languish, feeling that their lives are empty. People who flourish experience extraordinary levels of well-being, psychologically and socially. Interestingly, they also tend to do good for others. They are engaged in the world, with their families, and with their work. They have a sense of purpose, and they share and celebrate what is good (Fredrickson, 2009).

It is important to note that well-being is not just about psychological factors. It depends in good measure on economic development and the functioning of social institutions and the communities in which we live. There are many studies that compare levels of well-being in different countries and the places in the world. They show that the people who live in the most developed nations, democracies, and places where they feel safe and looked after by their governments tend to be happier and more satisfied with their lives.

The relationship between economics and psychological well-being is complex. Diener & Biswas-Diener (2008), after doing an overview of many studies on the topic, conclude that money can buy happiness to a certain point, given that wealthier people tend to be more satisfied with their lives and citizens of developed countries tend to be happier than the inhabitants of poor nations.[12] Still, the authors point out, these averages do not apply to everyone; there are some very poor people who are very happy and some unhappy millionaires. What research suggests is that having more money brings moderate improvements in levels of happiness. When you have very little, an increase in your income brings a big increment in your level of happiness; when you have a greater income, having more money only increases your happiness slightly. Diener and Biswas-Diener (2008) explain that, more than our absolute income, our expectations and attitudes about material goods are what have the greatest impact on our happiness. They conclude that, in general, it is good for happiness to have money, but it is toxic for happiness to want money too much (2008, p.111).

---

[12] This is a trend, but there are exceptions. For example, some countries in Latin America have higher levels of happiness than their economic indicators would predict. (Buettner, 2010)

Exercise 3.5 Research Your Country's Levels of Happiness and Well-Being

There are many ways to measure life satisfaction, happiness and well-being, and many organizations that research these topics. Dan Buettner in his book *Thrive* (2010) mentions the following:

World Data Base of Happiness

World Values Survey

Gallup World Poll

Latinobarómetro

Eurobarometer

Be a researcher for a few minutes and explore these websites. Write down some of your reactions. What surprises or does not surprise you? What do you find intriguing?

_____

_____

_____

In his book, Flourishing, Martin Seligman predicts that by 2051, 51% of the world's population will be flourishing. He believes that when people flourish, health productivity and peace follow (2011, p. 4248-57). What do you think?

Conversation Exercise Week 3

Please get together with a friend or conversational partner. Talk about PERMA and the elements of well-being, particularly about your thoughts on positivity. Share your reactions and questions.

Readings for Week 3

Fredrickson, B. (2009). Positivity: Groundbreaking Research Reveals How to Embrace the Hidden Strength of Positive Emotions, Overcome Negativity, and Thrive. New York: Crown.

Seligman, M. E. (2011). Flourish: a visionary new understanding of happiness and well-being. New York, NY: Free Press. Chap.1

Additional Readings for Week 3

Buettner, D. (2010). Thrive. Finding Happiness the Blue Zones Way. Washington, D.C.: National Geographic Society. Chap.1

References

Buettner, D. (2010). Thrive. Finding Happiness the Blue Zones Way. Washington, D.C.: National Geographic Society.

Danner, D. D., Snowdon, D. A., & V. Friesen., W. (2001). Positive emotions in early life and longevity: Findings from the nun study. Journal of Personality and Social Psychology, 80, 804–813.

Diener, E., & Biswas-Diener, R. (2008). Happiness Unlocking the Mysteries of Psychological Wealth. Malden MA: Blackwell.

Fredrickson, B. (2009). Positivity: Groundbreaking Research Reveals How to Embrace the Hidden Strength of Positive Emotions, Overcome Negativity, and Thrive. New York: Crown.

Fredrickson, B. (2003). The Value of Positive Emotions. The emerging science of positive psychology is coming to understand why it's good to feel good. American Scientist, Vol.91. July-Aug 2003.

Harker, L., & Keltner, D. (2001). Expression of positive emotion in women's college yearbook pictures and their relationship to personality and life outcomes across adulthood. Journal of Personality and Social Psychology 80, 112-24.

Seligman, M. E. (2011). Flourish: a visionary new understanding of happiness and well-being. New York, NY: Free Press.

Week 4 Engagement: Discovering and Getting Reacquainted with your Special Skills and Strengths

According to Dr. Martin Seligman (2011,2002), one of the pillars of well-being and a factor that makes people "flourish" is their engagement in life. Living an engaged life means being actively involved in what we do, using our skills and our strengths in our work, at home and in our relationships with other people. This week, you will be exploring your special skills and the times when you have optimal or "flow" experiences. You will also be invited to discover, or get back in touch with, your character strengths and see what these contribute to your sense of who you are.

Flow Experiences

One of the founders of Positive Psychology is Dr. Mihaly Csikszentmihalyi, a professor at Claremont University. For over 40 years, he has studied people's experiences--what they do, think and feel as they go about their daily lives. He has also researched happiness, creativity and the development of the notion of "self." One of Csikszentmihalyi's most important contributions is the discovery of "flow experiences." We are "in flow" when we do activities that require total concentration, are challenging and require us to use and develop our skills. When we are in flow, we focus all of our attention and effort into what we are doing. Right then our emotional state generally is neutral, but after- wards we tend to feel satisfied, in a good mood and with stronger self-esteem (Wells, 1998). Csikszentmihalyi has found that the more we have flow experiences, the happier and more satisfied we are with our lives over the long run.

Exercise 4.1 Your Recent Flow Experiences [13]

Think of recent times when you were doing something and:

You lost track of time;

You were totally involved in the activity;

You were not self-conscious while you were doing it.

Write down 3 instances when this happened:

1. _____

2. _____

3. _____

Now think about the skills that are involved in each of these activities. Please write down at least one skill that you put into action when you had these flow experiences. For example, if you were in flow when you were teaching a class, some of the skills involved may include being eloquent, or having the ability to summarize and transmit concepts clearly. If you had a flow experience while you were dancing, some of your skills might be knowing how to do the swing, or hip hop, or having a sense of rhythm, etc.

1. _____

2. _____

3. _____

---

[13] If you cannot identify any recent experiences, look further into the past.

Something fascinating about flow experiences is how diverse they are. People can be in flow when they paint, play chess, knit, cook, run, swim, write a novel, solve a math problem, fix a car, do a cross word puzzle, play cards, observe a cell under a microscope or the stars in the sky. Almost any activity we can think of can be a source of flow. But something that puts you in flow may be totally uninteresting to someone else, or impossibly hard for another person.

Csikszentmihalyi has found that even though the "what" of flow experiences can be very different, the "how" we have them seems to be consistent. His research data on thousands of people all over the world show that there are certain conditions that are necessary to have a flow experience. These include:

1.   **Clear Goals** It is very important to know what we are trying to accomplish in an activity. For example, when we play basketball the goal is to get the ball through the hoop; if we are baking a cake, we need an idea of what it should look and taste like when it is ready; when a surgeon is making an incision, she knows what kind of operation she will be performing. Imagine sitting around a table with two other people, being given a deck of cards with only one instruction: "Play." Do you think you would have a flow experience? You would probably feel confused and frustrated. Chances are you would ask "play what?" You need to know the game you are expected to play, to understand its goals and rules, and then, maybe, you can get it going and enjoy it.

2.   **Feedback** We are more likely to have a flow experience when the activity gives us immediate feedback. For example, if you are cooking a stew and you taste it, you realize it does not have enough salt and you add some more. Or a golfer might be putting and be able to tell right away if the ball went too far or did not reach the hole, so he then adjusts his next stroke. A sailor can feel if the boat is leaning towards one side and do something to balance it again. The sooner we get feedback in an activity, the more likely it is that we will stay engaged in it.

3.   **The Right Proportion of Challenge and Skill** This is probably the most important condition for a flow experience: the relationship between how much skill we have for an activity and how challenging it is for us. Imagine that you are

an average tennis player. You have been playing almost every weekend for about five years. When you play with your tennis partner, who is about as good as you are for the sport, you often lose track of time and have a great time. But imagine they asked you and your partner to play against Rafael Nadal. How do you think you would feel? Or, if your sister asked you to play a match against her six-year-old son, what would the game be like for you? Csikszentmihalyi has discovered that if an activity is too easy for us (not enough of a challenge), we tend to feel bored, while if it is too hard for our level of skill (too challenging), we get anxious. When the combination of skill and challenge is "just right" we can have flow experiences. These usually happen when we have a moderate to high level of skill and we face a moderate to high level of challenge.

4.   **Deep Concentration** This is also a key feature of flow experiences. When we are totally focused on what we are doing, we feel as if we are one with the activity, we are not observing ourselves while we do it, nor judging our performance (we may evaluate the results after wards, but not right then). Csikszentmihalyi points out that the word "extasis" in Greek means "stepping aside" and likens that to a flow experience, in the sense that it is like stepping out of our ego and being entranced in what we do.

5.   **Being in the Present** This goes hand in hand with the full concentration described above. When we are totally engaged in an activity, we cannot get distracted and think about the past or the future, we have to be fully in the present moment. Imagine a pianist who is playing a concerto and starts to think about his next concert or about what he did last week. He would surely hit the wrong note and fall out of synch with the orchestra.

6.   **Distorted Perception of Time** If you had to describe flow in just one phrase, "experiencing a distorted perception of time" is what most people would probably say. When we are in flow, time generally seems to go by quickly (the proverbial "time flies when you are having fun"). Can you remember a time that you were working on something and when you looked at your clock you could not believe that it was already that late? In some cases, flow experiences make time seem to go very slowly, but they are less frequent than those when time seems to fly.

7.   **<u>Apparently Effortless Control</u>** When we have a flow experience, it may seem that we are not putting too much effort into controlling the activity. It is as if the activity takes on a life of its own, or that we are coordinated with it in a smooth way. Dancers have to rehearse for months, and when they finally perform on stage, they may feel that the ballet itself takes over. The same could be true for a football team, where players practice for a long time, repeating their moves over and over, and then experience flow during the final game. Have you heard the saying: "Practice, practice, practice, then be spontaneous?" I think it captures an important part of the flow experience. You need to rehearse and do things repeatedly to develop the skills that are necessary, and when you are actually engaged in the activity, you do so in the unique way that the situation requires.

Dr. Csïkszentmihalyi has even been able to map how different levels of skill and challenge correlate with different moods and states of mind. It is illustrated in the following diagram:

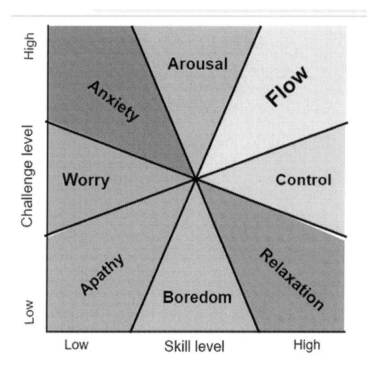

Diagram 1. Types of Experience According to Ratio of Skill and Challenge
Based on Csikszentmihalyi (2003)

To see how this framework applies to your own life, please do the following exercise:

Exercise 4.2 Non-Optimal and Optimal Experiences [14]

The term "Optimal Experience" is synonymous with "Flow." An optimal experience is a flow experience. A non-optimal experience can be any experience in the other quadrants in the diagram It might be a time when you felt bored, anxious or apathetic, for example.

A.   <u>**Non-Optimal Experiences**</u>

Think about the past few weeks and identify a time during which you felt anxious or bored and write it down.

_____

_____

1. What were you doing?

_____

_____

2. Where were you?

_____

_____

3. Whom were you with?

_____

_____

4. How challenging was this activity for you

1	2	3	4	5	6	7	8	9	10

1-Extremely Easy   **10-Extremely Hard**

---
[14] Based on the Experience Sampling Questionnaire developed by Csikszentmihalyi and collaborators.

5. How much skill do you feel you had for that activity?

| 1 | 2 | 3 | 4 | 5 | 6 | 7 | 8 | 9 | 10 |

1-No Skill   10-A Lot of Skill

B.   Optimal Experiences

Now think about the past few weeks and write down a time during which you feel you were in FLOW, when you were totally concentrated and maybe lost track of time.

_____

_____

1. What were you doing?

_____

_____

2. Where were you?

_____

_____

3. Who were you with?

_____

_____

4. How challenging was this activity for you

| 1 | 2 | 3 | 4 | 5 | 6 | 7 | 8 | 9 | 10 |

1-Extremely Easy   10-Extremely Hard

5. How much skill do you feel you had for that activity?

| 1 | 2 | 3 | 4 | 5 | 6 | 7 | 8 | 9 | 10 |

1-No Skill   10-A Lot of Skill

Reflection

What do you think after examining some of your optimal and non-optimal experiences?

_____

_____

_____

_____

_____

Researchers who study flow think that it is important for people to know what activities create optimal experiences for them and to deliberately create opportunities for flow in their lives.

An interesting aspect of flow is that it is not static. It is a dynamic process. You may have flow experiences for some time when you are at a certain level of skill, but this can change if your skills improve and the challenge doesn't increase. For example, if you are learning to play the piano, in the beginning even a simple piece can be challenging and you can feel anxious. Once you learn how to play it, you may be in flow every time you play it for a few weeks. But after a while, as your piano playing technique develops, the piece may become boring. Then you will need to tackle a more difficult song, which will be hard initially and later you may "flow" with it. And so on and so forth. In order to have flow experiences, we constantly need to adjust our skills and the challenges we face.

As Csikszentmihalyi (1997) points out, we cannot be in a constant state of flow. We all need to do some things that are not particularly stimulating or that we do not enjoy. We are often stressed when we face tasks for which we are not apt or prepared. We have to sleep and do maintenance work on ourselves and our homes. Still, it seems that many people could use more flow in their lives. There are studies conducted by the Gallup Organization that report that about one in five adults in Europe and the US say that he/she never has flow experiences, while another 20% have them every day. Most people, between 60 and 70%, occasionally have optimal experiences (between once every few months and once a week). If you had to answer that survey, how often would you say you have flow experiences? Csikszentmihalyi invites us to ask ourselves: Knowing the kind of person that I am, the interests and skills I have, what are the most rewarding flow activities for me (1993)?

I have met many people who get a little nostalgic when they think about flow in their lives. They say things like, "I used to love playing the guitar, but I don't have time anymore." or "I was really good with languages, but stopped taking classes because I had to work," or "I used to really like drawing, but I thought it would be childish to do it now".

Exercise 4.3 My History of Flow

Take a trip down memory lane and try to remember what kinds of flow experiences you had during different times of your life. What activities were you very engaged in when you were a child, a teenager, or young adult. What made you lose track of time and feel good afterwards?

Here is a time line to help you recall some your earlier flow experiences. You do not need to fill every age bracket, just the ones that come to mind most vividly.

Stage of My Life	Activities That Were Flow Experiences For Me
Young Child	_____
Teenager	_____
Young Adult	_____
Adult	_____
Middle Aged	_____
Mature Adult	_____
Older Adult	_____

Reflection

What are you thinking and feeling after doing this exercise?

_____

_____

_____

_____

Let me share with you the story of Eduardo [15], who came to see me for consultation because he felt he had lost his "zest for life." Many things were going on at that point for him. His parents were aging and in bad health, he had some mild medical problems himself, and he was not finding much satisfaction in his current work. He had retired early and started a small part time business of his own. He liked the fact that he was his own boss, but he felt very isolated and bored. He did not feel he had any challenges in what he did because the business was simple and "ran itself." His old job was more interesting, and he had very good relationships with his coworkers, with whom he also socialized often. Since he often spoke of feeling bored, I asked him to write a list of experiences that had brought him satisfaction in life.

When we had our next meeting, the first item on his list was so fascinating that we spent the whole hour talking about it. It said "building my Oriental City." He explained that when he was a little boy, he lived with his family in a small town that had a tile factory where his father worked. They did not have much money to buy toys, but he liked to collect little pieces of tile that he found on the ground near the factory and use them to build things. When he was about ten, he decided that he wanted to build an Oriental city with pagodas, temples, and modern buildings like the ones he had in seen in a movie and in a book. Every day after school, Eduardo would work on his city. "I would build and build and almost every night my mother would call me for supper and I could not believe the afternoon had already passed. I would lose track of time whenever I was working on my project."

---

[15] Not his real name.

The city was so pretty and grew so large that Eduardo's parents graciously let him move the furniture from the living room so the city could expand. Soon the other children in the town would come to admire it and Eduardo's parents graciously let them visit.

When Eduardo recalled how whole afternoons would go by and he did not feel the time pass, of course I thought of "flow." I asked him if he had ever heard about this concept. He hadn't, but said he wanted to know, so I drew a diagram similar to the one you saw earlier. Eduardo seemed very interested. I happened to have a copy of Finding Flow in my office, so I lent it to him and he took it home.

The following week Eduardo said that the book had helped him realize that he used to have many flow experiences in the past, but he no longer did. He remembered that he and his best friend used to restore old cars. It was fun and challenging to figure out how to repair them, paint them and accessorize them. Eduardo mentioned that he had gone over his list of twenty-one examples of satisfying experiences and realized that there was a pattern. Many of the events that had made him feel very good had to do with building, inventing, and repairing things. As a teenager, he would collect discarded bicycles and make them work again. In college he "built" a student organization. As an adult, he had rebuilt by himself the house where he and his family lived. His Oriental City was the most vivid example of his love of building and creativity.

Based on this, we talked about ways in which he could have more flow experiences and start "building" again. He decided to make his business more interesting by offering a repair service to his clients and do the repairs himself. And he took other steps to be more engaged in his social and family life. After a few sessions, he felt that his zest for life was back (Tarragona, 2008)

When they think about their earlier flow experiences, many people wish they could re-claim the kinds of activities and skills that put them in flow in their childhood or youth. David Epston, one of the most important narrative practitioners and authors, developed an interview to explore some of the special skills we had as children and teenagers. Here is an adaptation of this exercise [16]. If you can, do it with a friend and interview each other. If you would rather do it alone, ask yourself these questions and write down the answers.

Exercise 4 Interview about your Special Skills as a Child or Adolescent
(Based on Epston, D. 1997)

1.   **What special skills did you have when you were about 9, 12 or 16 years old? (You   pick an age.)**

_____

_____

2.   **What joys and satisfactions did these skills bring you?**

_____

_____

3.   **Can you remember an adult (mother, father, uncle, aunt, grandparent, teacher, etc.) who knew you and really appreciated these skills?**

_____

_____

4.   **How did that adult show that he/she knew you had that skill?**

_____

_____

5.   **If you, as you are now, could have been available for your_____year-old self, what would you have said or done to show your appreciation for those skills?**

_____

_____

---

[16] Based on Epston (1997)

6.   Have you continued to nurture or develop those skills? If you have, how have you done it? Have these long-nurtured skills had impact on your sense of who you are?

_____

_____

7.   Do you remember having suppressed or renounced some of those skills at some point in your life? If you did, how did that happen? Has the absence of these skills in your life had an effect for you?

_____

_____

8.   As an adult, have you considered getting reacquainted with any of those skills? If so, how could you start to do it? Why would this be important for you?

_____

_____

Reflections

What are you thinking and feeling after doing this interview?

_____

_____

_____

_____

_____

_____

_____

_____

Flow experiences rarely happen out of the blue. Most of the time, we have to cultivate them. We cannot guarantee that something will get us into flow, but we can create the conditions that make it more likely. Some of the things we can do to have more flow in our lives include:

1. **Learn to focus and control our attention**, concentrating as much as we can on everything we do, even if it is routine activity.[17] (Csikszentmihalyi, 1997)

2. **Keep a diary of everything we do during the day for a couple of weeks.** It is useful if we also note how we felt during the day and at the end of it. Doing this can help us see if there are patterns of how certain activities, places and people correlate with our states of mind. (Csikszentmihalyi, 1997).

3. **Take our leisure time seriously.** Dr. Csikszentmihalyi stresses that one way to have more flow is to plan and structure our free time as carefully as we do our work time. This may sound counter intuitive, you may think: I love having nothing to do and just "chilling" during the little free time that I have. Relaxing is indeed important and we need to devote some time to it (many people do this by watching TV, for example), but Csikszentmihalyi has found that we get more enjoyment from activities that bring us satisfaction (that require some skills, present some challenge and are meaningful). He encourages us to observe if we feel different after doing a complex flow activity (like skiing, reading a good book or a stimulating conversation) than we do after watching TV (Csikszentmihalyi, 1993, p. 205)

4. **Foster flow at work.** You may be one of the lucky people who really enjoy their work, but even if you are not, you can try experimenting with skills and challenges to get closer to the flow "zone": make your tasks more challenging if you tend to feel bored, or develop your skills, if you tend to feel anxious about what you have to do on the job (Lyubomirsky, 2008, Miller & Frisch, 2009, Csikszentmihalyi, 1997).

5. **Find flow in relationships.** Our relationships with other people are very important sources of flow in our lives. Csikszentmihalyi points out that when two people are relating, they are paying attention to each other, they may have a common goal, and they

---

[17] This is very connected to mindfulness. There is a wonderful workbook about Mindfulness in this series: Positively Mindful, by Donald Altman.

enjoy their interaction. Can you think of a time when you were speaking with someone for hours? Csikszentmihalyi says that the flow of conversation is one of the best things in life (1997). I couldn't agree more. Try to learn something from each person, to be curious about them, and chances are the conversation will flow.

We have seen that flow experiences contribute to happiness in our lives, but what do they have to do with identity, or on this case, with your preferred identity? Csikszentmihalyi (1993, p. 237) says that "every flow experience contributes to the growth of the self". Flow experiences help us develop our uniqueness, to structure and give order to our experience, and to develop psychological complexity. This complexity of conscious- ness "involves becoming aware of and in control of one's unique potentials, and being able to create harmony between goals and desires, sensations and experience, both for oneself and for others" (Csikszentmihalyi, 1993, pp. 207-208)

Think about this: How does knowing about your skills, goals and desires contribute to your sense of who you are? How would you say your recent flow experience can con- tribute to your identity?

Character Strengths

Another important aspect of living an engaged life is being aware of and using our strengths. Actually, our strengths of character are intertwined with every aspect of our well-being (Seligman M. E., 2011). I think of this as being able to bring the best of who we are into our activities and our relationships. In recent years there has been a tremendous growth in strengths-based approaches in management, therapy, coaching, education and other fields. Positive psychology has made important contributions to these areas, since it offers a scientific approach to learning about human strengths.

Martin Seligman, Christopher Peterson and their collaborators (Peterson & Seligman, 2004, Seligman M. E., 2005) have compiled a list of personal characteristics that:

- Are valued in most cultures throughout the world;
- Are valued in and of themselves (not just as a means to an end);
- Can be developed or nurtured.

These strengths are different from talents. Talents tend to be automatic or innate and are often associated with physical or cognitive skills, like having perfect speech or being a very fast runner. Character strengths have to do with moral qualities; they depend more on our volition. For example, we can decide to be more disciplined, or more just, and work to develop these character strengths (while we can't decide to have good arches in our feet for ballet or to have a photographic memory).

Researchers (Seligman M. E., 2002, Peterson & Seligman, 2004, Dahlsgaard, Peterson, & Seligman, 2005) have found 24 strengths of character that are almost universally recognized and valued and that are present in the literature and traditions of many cultures throughout history. They propose that these character strengths can be grouped in six broad categories or virtues:

1. <u>**Wisdom**</u> - Which includes creativity, curiosity, judgment/open-mindedness, love of learning, perspective;

2. <u>**Courage**</u> - Which includes bravery, perseverance and honesty;

3. <u>**Justice**</u> - Which includes teamwork, fairness and leadership;

4. <u>**Humanity**</u> – Which refers to love, kindness and social intelligence;

5. <u>**Temperance**</u> - Which includes forgiveness, humility, prudence and self-regulation;

6. <u>**Transcendence**</u> - Which includes appreciation of beauty and excellence, gratitude, hope, humor, spirituality/religiousness and zest.

Christopher Peterson and Nansook Park, professors of psychology at the University of Michigan, found that these character strengths are distributed in distinct ways among American people and that they are correlated to age, gender and political ideology, among other things. For example, older people tend to be more religious, while younger people show more sense of humor (Peterson, 2008). Park & Peterson have also seen that the most frequent strengths of children are their capacity to love, curiosity and sense of humor, while they are not very modest and, as we would expect, they tend not to be able to put things in perspective nor to forgive (2006). Every day there are more studies that look at character strengths in different countries and cultures (Park, Peterson & Seligman, 2006; Park, Peterson & Ruch, 2009).

Peterson and Park have also looked at character strengths in families. The most salient ones are justice, forgiveness, honesty, teamwork, and social intelligence (Peterson,

2008). They (Peterson & Park, 2006) have also found that some strengths have particularly high correlations with satisfaction at work and with overall satisfaction with life: curiosity, zest, gratitude, hope and the capacity to love.

In Chapter 1 we talked about "dominant narratives" or ways of talking and thinking that have a strong influence on how we think and what we do. These dominant narratives exist not only at an individual level, but more broadly in cultures and societies. One very powerful narrative in our contemporary Western world has to do with pathology. More and more aspects of human experience are seen as abnormal or pathological.

Peterson and Seligman (2004) wanted to counterbalance the excessive emphasis on pathology that psychology has had, and they wrote Character Strengths and Virtues: A Handbook and Classification, which they see as a DSM[18] of human strengths and virtues, a "manual of the sanities." Christopher Peterson also developed a questionnaire to assess people's character strengths. It has been answered by over one million people all over the world (Seligman M. E., 2011) The instrument is called the "VIA Survey of Character Strengths," is available online, free of charge, through the Authentic Happiness Website, www.authentichappiness.sas.upenn.edu, or through the VIA Institute on Character http://www.viacharacter.org/SURVEY.

There are other ways to think about strengths and different tests to measure them, some for a fee. The Realise2 measure, for example, which was developed by the CAPP team in the UK is available at http://www.cappeu.com/, and the StrengthsFinder2 from the Gallup Organization, which you can find at (http://www.strengthsfinder.com).

As you read the list of character strengths, did you start to think about your own? How well do you know your strengths of character? Are you curious about them? I hope so because this is your next exercise:

---

[18] Diagnostic and Statistical Manual of Mental Disorders, a book that contains more than 200 classifications of mental disturbances.

Exercise 4.5 Your Character Strengths

A.   Please go online and take the VIA Survey of Character Strengths (long version)[19], available free of charge at http://www.viacharacter.org/SURVEY or at www.authentichappiness.sas.upenn.edu. The two versions are identical and take about 45 minutes to complete.

B.   Get your results and print them.

C.   Write down your top five strengths according to this test.
       My top five strengths are:

       _____

       _____

       _____

       _____

       _____

Seligman and Peterson use the term "signature strengths" to refer to the strengths that people recognize, exercise and celebrate. They are characterized by a sense of authenticity (they describe the "real me"), a feeling of excitement when displaying them, a rapid learning curve as the strength is put into action, a desire to use it in different ways, a feeling that we can't help but use that strength, having projects that revolve around it, and feeling joy and enthusiasm when we use it (Peterson & Seligman, 2004,Seligman M. E., 2011).

Reflection

What was it like for you to answer the strengths survey?

_____

_____

[19] If you prefer, you can take the Realise2 or the Strengths Finder2 tests (for a fee): http://www.cappeu.com/ and www.strengthsfinder.com, respectively.

What do you think of the results?

_____

_____

Do you feel they reflect some of your signature strengths?

_____

_____

Are they what you would have predicted?

_____

_____

If so, why?

_____

_____

If not, which strengths would you have thought would come out highest?

_____

_____

Did you find anything particularly intriguing orsurprising?

_____

_____

Practitioners and academics agree on the importance of knowing and using our strengths. Researchers have designed "positive interventions." which are exercises or activities that have the explicit purpose of increasing a person's well-being and have been shown to be effective experimentally. One of the positive interventions that has proven to be most powerful has to do with strengths. It involves taking a personal strength and deliberately using it in a different way for one week. Doing this improves people's mood and life satisfaction in a way that lasts for several months. This was found in controlled research studies and it was true even for people who were depressed (Seligman, Steen, Park & Peterson, 2005, Seligman M. E., 2011).

How would you be to use a strength differently? It is best for each person to design that, but let me give you a couple of examples. Say one of your top strengths is appreciation of beauty and you tend to use it by listening to music. This week you may want to spend every lunch hour in a park observing beauty in Nature. If one of your strengths is humor and you realize you mostly demonstrate it during weekends with your friends, you may try posting a cartoon on the office bulletin board every day at work. Would you like to use one of your signature strengths differently this week? If so, which one? Any ideas how you might go about it?

Narrative and constructionist practitioners sometimes are not too fond of the term "strength" because it can be understood as something that you either have or you do not have "inside you," almost as if a strength was a substance and the person the container of that substance. From narrative and constructionist perspectives, all of our experiences are conceptualized as relational and people are seen agents who are constantly creating their identity. I believe we can think about strengths in a relational way and see ourselves as active constructors of these strengths.

The final exercise for this chapter invites you to further explore your strengths and the role they play in your identity and your relationships.

Exercise 4.6 Interview about Strengths in Your Life
(inspired by Freedman, Combs & M. White)

Write your top 3 of signature strengths:

_____,_____, _____

Of these 3, which one seems more evident in your daily life these days?

_____

Do you think other people notice this strength in you? Has anyone mentioned any-thing about it? (Who? What did he/she say?) If nobody has noticed it, what would they need to know about you to realize that this is an important strength in your life?

_____

_____

_____

_____

When did you start to realize this could be an important strength in your life? Can you remember a particular incident?

_____

_____

_____

_____

_____

Can you tell me an anecdote or story that illustrates this strength in action?

_____

_____

_____

_____

_____

_____

What impact has this strength had in your life?

_____

_____

_____

_____

_____

_____

How do you nurture and embody this strength?

_____

_____

_____

_____
_____
_____
_____

In which of your relationships is this strength more evident? Who helps you perform this strength? How?

_____
_____
_____
_____
_____
_____

If you continue to develop and use this strength, what effect do you think it may have in your life in the future?

_____
_____
_____
_____
_____
_____

Reflection

What are you feeling and thinking after doing this exercise?

_____
_____
_____
_____
_____
_____

Martin Seligman says "I do not believe that you should devote overly much effort to correcting your weaknesses. Rather, I believe that the highest success in living and the highest emotional satisfaction comes from building and using our signature strengths" (2002, p.13). Do you agree?

Conversation Exercise Week 4:

Please get together with a friend or conversational partner. Talk about your signature strengths. Commit to use one of your strengths differently in the coming week and help each other brainstorm about how you will do it.

Readings for Week 4

Csikszentmihalyi, M. (1997). Finding flow: the psychology of engagement with everyday life. . New York: Basic Books.

Nakamura J. & Csikszentmihalyi ,M. (2005) The Concept of Flow. In Snyder, C.R. & Lopez, S.J.1. Handbook of Positive Psychology, New York: Oxford University Press, pp. 89-105.

Further Readings for Week 4

Csikszentmihalyi, M. (1990). Flow. The psychology of optimal experience . New York. Harper & Row.

Tarragona, M. (2008). Postmodern and Post-structuralist Therapies. In J. Lebow, Twenty-first Century Psychotherapies (pp. 167-205). Hoboken, NJ: Wiley. Read the case study for a more detailed account of how flow was a central aspect of a therapeutic process.

Sin, Nancy L. & Lyubomirsky, S. (2009) Enhancing Well Being and Alleviating Depressive Symptoms with Positive Psychology Interventions. Journal of Clinical Psychology: In Session. Vol. 65(5) 467-487

References

Altman, D. Positively Mindful Skills Concepts and Research.

Csikszentmihalyi, M. (1997). Finding flow: the psychology of engagement with every-day life. New York: Basic Books.

Csikszentmihalyi, M. (1993). The evolving self: a psychology for the third millennium. New York, NY: HarperCollins Publishers.

Dahlsgaard, K., Peterson, C. C., & Seligman, M. (2005). Dahlsgaard, K. Shared Virtue: The convergence of valued human strengths across culture and history. Review of General Psychology, 9, 203-213.

Miller, C. A., & Frisch, M. B. (2009). Creating your best life: the ultimate life list guide. New York: Sterling.

Nakamura, J. & Csikszentmihalyi, M. (2005). The concept of flow. In, C.R. Snyder and S.J. Lopez (eds). Handbook of Positive Psychology New York: Oxford University Press, pp. 89-105.

Park, N., & Peterson, C. (2006). (2006). Character strengths and happiness among young children: Content Analysis of parental descriptions. Journal of Happiness Studies, 7, 323–341.

Park, N., Peterson, C., & Ruch, W. (2009). Orientation to happiness: National comparisons. Journal of Positive Psychology. 4, 273–279.

Peterson, C. (2008). Lecture Notes Positive Psychology Immersion Course. Mentor Coach.

Peterson, C., & Seligman, M. (2004). Character Strengths and Virtues: A Handbook and Classification. New York: Oxford University Press.

Seligman, M. E. (2002). Authentic happiness: using the new positive psychology to realize your potential for lasting fulfillment. New York: Free Press.

Seligman, M. E. (2011). Flourish: a visionary new understanding of happiness and well-being. . New York, NY: Free Press.

Seligman, M. E. (2005). Positive Psychology Progress Empirical Validation of Interventions. American Psychologist, 410-421.

Tarragona, M. (2008). Postmodern and Post-structuralist Therapies. In J. Lebow, Twenty-first Century Psychotherapies (pp. 167-205). Hoboken, NJ: Wiley.

Wells, A. J. (1998). Auto Estima y Experiencia Óptima. In M. Csikszentmihalyi, & I. Csikszentmihalyi, Experiencia Óptima Estudios Psicológicos del Flujo en la Conciencia (pp. 319-332). Bilbao: Desclée De Brouwer.

Wylie, M. S. (1994, Nov/Dec). Panning for gold. Family Therapy Networker, 40-48.

This week we will look at some of the research findings about the importance that interpersonal relationships have for our well-being. Then I will invite you to explore how your relationships contribute to your identity and to think about how you can nurture and develop relationships that fit with your preferred ways of being.

Other People Matter

Dr. Christopher Peterson, one of the most important researchers in the field, says that positive psychology can be summarized in three words: "Other People Matter." I love this definition and it fits very well with a relational view of identity. Peterson points out that the variable that correlates most consistently with well-being is the quality our relationships. Martin Seligman considers positive relationships one of the central elements of well-being and human flourishing (2011).

Mihaly Csikszentmihalyi, of whom we spoke so much in the previous chapter, designed a creative way to learn about people's everyday activities, thoughts and feelings. It is called the Experience Sampling Method. Participants in a study are given a cell phone and they are "beeped" randomly about eight times a day for a week. When they receive the beep they have to answer a quick survey on their screen that asks about where they are, whom they are with, how they are feeling, how engaged they are in the activity, etc. This way, researchers can get "snapshots" of people's experiences. Many of their findings highlight the role that other people play in our emotional life. Over many years and in different countries, Experience Sampling studies have repeatedly shown that people tend to get sad when they are alone and revive when they are with others (Csikszentmihalyi, 1997) [20] (Diener & Biswas-Diener, 2008). Csikszentmihalyi's research has even shown that the moods of people who were diagnosed with chronic depression or eating disorders were indistinguishable from those of healthy people, as long as they were in the company of others and doing something that requires concentration (1997).

---

[20] He has also found that people need some solitude and that there is an optimum amount of "alone time" for our well-being, but in general we are happier when we are accompanied.

Remember all we said about flow in Chapter 4? For Csikszentmihalyi, these findings indicate that the presence of another person makes us concentrate our attention, it creates goals (Even in "superficial" interactions there are goals, such as being courteous, creating or maintaining a connection, and finding a conversation topic.) and it gives us feedback. For example, Csikszentmihalyi has found that people are in their best moods when they are with their friends. This is true not just for teenagers, but for retirees in their 80's as well. Friendship plays a big part in our quality of life, throughout our lifetime. In general, people's moods are okay when they are with their families—not as good as when they are with their friends, but fairly good. (Csikszentmihalyi, 1997).

These are just a few examples that illustrate Peterson's assertion that other people matter. Diener and Biswas-Diener (2008) summarize why relationships matter. They allow us to love and to be loved, offer help and support, stimulate our minds and challenge us to form our ideas, give us a sense of belonging, and are just plain fun.

Love and Relationships

Barbara Fredrickson specializes in studying positive emotions and their effects in our lives. She has found that there are ten forms of positivity: joy, gratitude, serenity, curiosity, hope, pride, fun, inspiration, awe and love. All of these are important for us to flourish, but love encompasses all the others. Fredrickson has found that love is the positive emotion that people experience most frequently (Fredrickson, 2009). Love changes the chemistry of our nervous system. For example, when we have social contact, and especially when we have physical contact,

we produce a hormone called oxytocin, which fosters bonding. Some people call it the "hug hormone" because women produce it during childbirth and breastfeeding. Interestingly, there is evidence that the father's levels of oxytocin also increase during the woman's pregnancy and continues to rise as he spends time with the baby. Oxytocin is associated with a neurotransmitter called dopamine. Dopamine plays an important role in the regulation of pleasure. Studies done with brain imaging procedures have found that people who say they are "very much

in love" show different patterns of brain activity when they see a picture of their partner than when they see picture of other loved ones, such as friends or family members (Bartels & Zeki, 2000).

These examples of the neurochemical aspects of love do not mean that it a purely biological phenomenon, but they suggest that we are predisposed or "wired" to love and to form relationships. The famous "monkey experiments" done 50 years ago by the psychologist Harry Harlow (1958) illustrate this. Dr. Harlow was trying to understand if babies developed a relationship with their mothers just because they needed them to provide food. He designed an experiment in which he separated baby monkeys from their mothers and put them in a cage with two mannequins. One was hard, made of wire, but dispensed milk; the other did not provide milk, but it was soft, made of terry cloth. His surprising findings were that little monkeys spent more time with the soft mannequin than with the one that dispensed milk. Harlow concluded that "warm contact" was as important as food for development. These studies paved the way for later research on attachment, a field that has grown enormously in recent years.

 Dr. George Vaillant has led the longest study of adult development ever conducted (the Harvard Adult Development Study). They have followed a cohort of men and women for over 70 years. After carefully looking into tens of factors that predict well-being in older adults, Vaillant has found that, without a doubt, relationships with others are what matters more than any- thing else. For example, participants in the study who had had warm and solid relationships had much greater probabilities of being successful at work, higher incomes and good health.
That is why Vaillant goes as far as saying: "Happiness is love. Period." (Vaillant, 2009)

"Love" does not refer only to couple hood, but to relationships in many areas of life—with our friends, children, family members and co-workers. There is evidence about the influence of friends on our well-being. Relationships at work seem to be particularly important. The Gallup surveys on well-being (Rath & Harter., 2010) found that people who have a "best friend" at work are more engaged in what they do; they produce better quality work and have fewer accidents on the job. Rath & Hater (2010) recommend trying to spend 6 hours a day with other people, strengthening our connections with our family members, friends, neighbors and co- workers and combining social contact with physical activity (such as going for a walk with a friend instead of to a coffee shop).

The Importance of Our Relationship Networks

Two dear colleagues of mine from Brazil, Marilene Grandesso and Marcia Volponi, do community therapy with large groups of people. One of the main purposes of this work is for people to expand and strengthen their social networks and sense of community in order to deal with their difficulties and problems. To illustrate the importance of social networks, Marcia told me a Brazilian saying that I have remembered ever since: "If you want to kill a spider, destroy its web."

Without its web, a spider can't survive. And the same is true for people. Today we know that interpersonal relationships are fundamental for well-being, both psychologically and physically. A group of researchers from Brigham Young University analyzed the results of 148 studies done in the course of 30 years, in which over 300,000 people participated (Holt-Lunstad, Byron Smith, & Layton, 2010). They wanted to see which variables correlated the most with mortality. The results were surprising. For both men and women of all ages, social support correlated with having a longer life. People who had good relationships with their friends, family members and communities had 50% fewer chances of dying during the time the study was conducted. Not having a social network carries a risk comparable to smoking or being overweight (House, Landis, & Umberson, 1988). Studies show that there is consistent evidence of a relationship be- tween social relationships and physical health, particularly in terms of the cardiovascular, hormonal and immune systems. People with few social bonds have almost twice the risk of dying of heart disease than people with strong social networks, and they are also twice as likely to get colds (Uchino, Cacioppo, & Kiecolt-Glaser, 1996).

If our relationships with others can impact our bodies, think of their importance for our emotional lives. There is a strong correlation between the quality of our relationships and our happiness. When researchers studied very happy people, the happiest among the happy, they found that they all had one thing in common: good relationships (Peterson, 2008, 2006). It sounds like such a cliché to say that we are social beings, but it is true!

Exercise 5.1 Your Web [21]

After reading about the importance of our networks, think about your web of relationships: Who are some of the people that support you, help you out when you need them? Whom do you spend your time with? With whom do you have fun? Who are important components of the net that help you survive and thrive? Write their names on this picture:

Reflection

What are you thinking and feeling after populating your web?

_____

_____

_____

Our Friends Can Be Contagious

Some of the most intriguing research about relationships has to do with social contagion. There is evidence that emotions can spread. We tend to synchronize our moods with those of people around us and our emotions mutually affect each other. Scientists have discovered that interpersonal relationships have an impact, not only on how we feel, but also on our goals and expectations. Fowler and Christakis (2008) conducted a fascinating study at Harvard University. They followed a group of 12,000 people for over 30 years and found that the probability of someone being happy was directly related to the happiness of the people to whom that person was connected. Having frequent social contact with a happy person increases our chances of being happy by 15%.[22]

One unexpected finding was that even "second hand" relationships can affect us. If your friend has a friend who is happy, not only do the chances of your friend being happy go up, but yours do, too, even if you do not know that person. Dr. Christakis, one of the researchers, says that these findings highlight that happiness is not just an individual matter, but that we are all part of a web of connections in which everyone's well-being influences everybody else. Other studies by the same authors show that negative behaviors are contagious as well. If you have a direct relationship with a smoker, your chances of smoking increase. And they increase if a friend of your friend smokes, even if you do not have a relationship with this other person.

---

[22] The statistical methods that Fowler and Christakis used have been questioned recently. I decided to keep their studies in this book because I think that, even if the effects of social contagion turn out to be less dramatic, it's existence is documented and it can be a useful concept to help us reflect bout how other people influence us in our lives.

Quitting smoking follows the same pattern. As smoking has become less acceptable in the workplace, people have quit smoking at home and with their friends too. If your best friend exercises a lot, you triple the odds that you will be physically active as well, and if your closest friend eats a healthy diet, your chances of doing the same increase five-fold. This is so important that researchers conclude that the people that we live with, such as our friends, may have a greater impact on our health than our family history of illness. (Rath & Harter., 2010)

Exercise 5.2 Contagion towards Your Preferred Self

After reading about social contagion, do you think you have ever experienced a social influence that was positive for you? If you have, what was it?

_____

_____

Think about two behaviors that you would like to increase or introduce in your life because they fit well with your preferred identity. What would these two behaviors be?

_____

_____

If you could "catch" these behaviors from some people in your life, who would they be?

_____

_____

If people wanted to "catch" a behavior they value from you, what could it be?

_____

Styles of Response in Relationships

We all know how important it is to have supportive relationships when we are going through hard times. But Dr. Shelly Gable and her team have discovered that good times are just as important, since we share positive experiences with others 80% of our days. Their research shows that a key element in satisfying relationships is how we react to the positive events in the other person's life (Gable, Reis, Impett, & Asher, 2004). They have classified people's responses according to two aspects: whether the response is active or passive, and whether it is constructive or destructive. So, a response can be active-constructive, active-destructive, passive-constructive or passive-destructive. Say, for example, that Johnny comes home and tells his mother that he got the lead role in the school play. This table shows the four possible types of responses on Mom's part:

Response Styles

	Active	Passive
Constructive	Mom jumps from her seat, hugs Johnny and says, "Yeah! Congratulations! You deserve it; you have worked so hard for this. We have to celebrate!"	Mom continues working on her computer, briefly glances at John and says, "That's nice, honey."
Destructive	Mom gets up from her desk, puts her hand on her hip, and sternly tells Johnny, "Well, I hope you realize what you are getting yourself into. You won't have time to do your homework and we know how hard the 8th grade is!"	Mom does not look up from the screen and mumbles, "Hmm, it was about time."

You can probably guess that the response that correlates with happier relationships is the Active-Constructive one.

Exercise 5.3 Sharing your Good News

Think of a recent time when you shared some good news with someone.

What did you share? Whom did you share it with?

_____

_____

How did this person respond?

_____

_____

Did his/her response correspond to any of the types described above? If so, which one?

_____

_____

What effect did this response have on you?

_____

_____

Marriage and Couple Hood

For many people, one of the most important relationships in life is marriage. There is evidence that the quality of a marriage has an effect on the well-being of the partners. In one study, researchers took 42 married couples to a hospital, they made small wounds on the participants' arms and measured the speed at which they healed. They found that people with hostility in their relationship took twice as long to heal than those who had good relationships. (Rath & Harter., 2010). Other studies support the idea that marriage correlates with health only when it is a fulfilling relationship (Kiecolt-Glaser & Newton, 2001). The data about the relationship between marriage and happiness is not clear cut. Diener and Biswas-Diener (2008) point out that even though on average married people are happier than singles, averages can blur differences. Some people are much happier after they marry, others are about as happy as before marriage and some are less so. What seems to matter is if the marriage is right for the person

One of the best-known researchers about relationships is Dr. John Gottman, of the University of Washington. For over 25 years, Gottman and his colleagues have been studying couples. They have developed a method to observe and code the interaction between partners that allows them to predict with 91% accuracy if a couple will stay together happily or will separate (Gottman & Silver, 1999).

Gottman has found that there are 4 kinds of interactions that predict bad outcomes for the relationship, which he calls "the four horsemen of apocalypse:" criticism, defensive-ness, contempt and "stonewalling". Criticism refers to making negative comments, complaining or blaming your partner. Defensiveness includes not being open to what your partner has to say, counter-attacking or whining. Contempt is a stronger form of criticism, showing disdain or disgust for your partner. Stonewalling happens when partners withdraw from the conversation and offer no feedback to each other. On the other side of the coin are the kinds of interactions that are frequent among happy couples: "soft start up", or the ability to begin talking about problems gently, turning towards each other (instead of turning away or against your partner), repairing conversations (an apology, a smile or humor to de-escalate a conflict), and accepting influence (being open to persuasion from your partner).

You may say that almost all couples have some amount of criticism or defensiveness, and you would be right. What Gottman and his team have found is that the presence of negative interactions is not very important in itself. What counts is the proportion or ratio of positive to negative interactions. Their data, obtained from thousands of participants, show that happy couples tend to have five positive interactions for every negative one. So, it is not that long-lasting couples never fight or criticize each other, but they have many more instances of appreciation and affection than of criticism or defensive- ness. There are couples who hardly ever argue, but if they do not have many positive interactions either, their marriage will probably not be very satisfying. Gottman says that the best predictor of success in marriage is that spouses have more positive than negative things to say about each other and to each other.

We have done a quick overview of some of the research findings on the importance of positive relationships for people's well-being. In the next section we will concentrate on how your relationships contribute to your identity.

Back to You, in Relationship

If you remember, in Chapters 1 and 2 we talked about a narrative view of self and identity, of how we can think of our sense of self as something that is maintained and trans- formed in our relationships with other people. Hopefully, doing the exercises in this chapter about your "web," social contagion, and your experiences with responses to good news has already got you thinking about important relationships in your life. I invite you to go into some of these relationships in more depth in the following exercises.

Exercise 5.4 Relational Identity Interview [23]

(Adapted from Freedman and Combs, 1999, and White & Epston, 1990)

Think about a person with whom you had a relationship that was positive and important to you (a friend, teacher, parent, child, partner).

Who was this person? Why was the relationship important for you?

_____

_____

_____

_____

Can you tell me a story or memorable experience from this relationship--an anecdote or vignette that would give me a sense of how you related to each other?

_____

_____

_____

_____

_____

_____

_____

_____

_____

---

[23] If you want to do this with a friend or conversational partner, please take turns interviewing each other. Go through the whole interview for one person first and then switch places.

What was important to you about this experience or event? What was important for the other person?

_____

_____

_____

_____

_____

_____

What do you think that this person most appreciated about you?

_____

_____

_____

_____

_____

_____

What aspects of yourself emerged or became apparent in this relationship?

_____

_____

_____

_____

_____

Did you find any pleasant surprises about yourself in this relationship?

_____

_____

_____

_____

_____

If I could interview this person, what would she/he tell me about you?

_____

_____

_____

_____

_____

How would you describe your identity in this relationship?

_____

_____

_____

_____

_____

If you could see yourself through that person's eyes, what would you appreciate most about how you are leading your life today?

_____

_____

_____

_____

_____

If you could keep that view of yourself near your heart for the next few weeks, what might be different in your life?

_____

_____

_____

_____

_____

Reflection

What are some of your thoughts and feelings after answering these questions?

_____

_____

_____

Identity as an Association

According to Michael White (2007), from a narrative perspective, identity can be understood as a group of relationships, an "association" or "club" of our life in which there are different members: significant people from our past, present and imagined future. The voices of these important figures in our lives contribute our construction of our identity. White proposed that we can decide who the members of the "club" of our life are, that we can upgrade them, honor their memberships or, in some cases, downgrade and even revoke them. White points out that these voices that shape our identity do not always have to be people we know, in some cases they may be authors of books we like, or characters from literature or film. White developed a particular way of interviewing that he called a "Re-membering Conversation", which invites people to think of their identity as multi-voiced, in contrast to the notion of identity as an "encapsulated self." He said, "In this multi-voiced sense of identity, people find that their lives are joined to the lives of others around shared and precious themes. This is a sense of identity that features positive, but non-heroic conclusions about one's actions in life and about who one is (White M. , 2007, p. 138)."

Re-membering conversations open the possibility of revising the membership of the club of our life, we can give more voice to those people whom we think make valuable contributions to our identity, based on our experiences and our relationships with them.

Exercise 5.5 Membership in Your "Life Association"

Adopt the metaphor that your life is like a club. You can decide who the members of this club are, based on how their voices and their relationships with you contribute to an identity that you like, to your preferred sense of self.

To get started, here are five membership cards. Please fill them out.

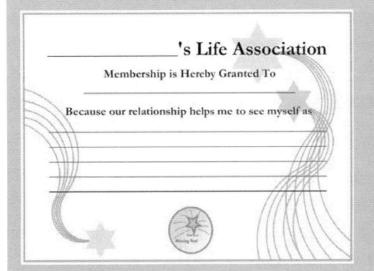

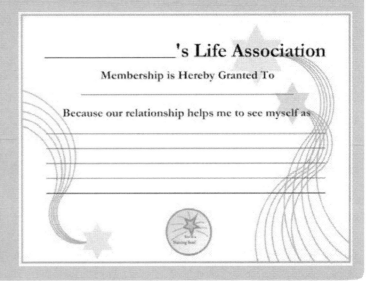

_____**'s Life Association**

Membership is Hereby Granted To

_____

Because our relationship helps me to see myself as

_____**'s Life Association**

Membership is Hereby Granted To

_____

Because our relationship helps me to see myself as

_____**'s Life Association**

Membership is Hereby Granted To

_____

Because our relationship helps me to see myself as

Reflection

If you keep this membership active, if you continue to nurture your relationships with these people, what effect do you think this may have on your identity and on your plans for the future?

Mutual Influence on Identities

Most relationships are two-way streets. An important aspect of narrative work is to explore how our lives are linked, how, if someone has had an effect on our life, chances are we have affected their life and identity too.

For example, Michael White (2007) shares the story of Jessica, a woman in her 40's who went to see him in therapy to consult about the consequences of abuse she had suffered when she was a child and teenager. Some of these consequences were that Jessica thought she was worthless and that her life had no hope. When Michael interviewed her, he realized she had survived many crises and wanted to understand what sustained her through these. Jessica then told him that she had managed to have a tiny bit of hope that her life would be better and that a neighbor had something to do with that hope. For about two years, Jessica had gone to this neighbor's house when she was hurting and the neighbor had comforted her, giving her food and introducing her to sewing and knitting. Michael asked Jessica what the neighbor might have seen in her that made her take her in, what she appreciated in Jessica. By answering these questions, Jessica voiced some different ideas about herself, seeing herself as worthy.

This could have been good enough, but White took another step in the reconstruction of Jessica's identity. He not only explored how this neighbor had impacted Jessica's life, he also asked questions about the contributions that Jessica had made to the neighbor. For example, what did she think that it meant for her neighbor that she (Jessica) had accepted her invitation to learn about knitting and sewing?

Let's try one final exercise in which we examine someone's contributions to your life and your contributions to his or her life:

Exercise 5.6 Mutual Influence

Let's go back to the person about whom you talked in the "Relational Identity" Exercise on page 100. Write his or her first name. _____

A.   <u>This Person's Influence in Your Life</u>

What would you say was the most important contribution that made in your life?

_____

_____

What is one positive change in your life that has to do with knowing?

_____

Can you tell me a story that would help me understand this change?

_____

_____

_____

_____

For you, what was the best part of the relationship with this person, something you will always carry with you?

_____

_____

_____

_____

B.   <u>Your Influence on This Person's Life</u>

What do you think_____would say was the most important contribution that you made to his/her life?

_____

_____

What is one positive change in_____'s life that has to do with knowing you?

_____

_____

_____

If I asked_____to tell me a story that would help me understand this change, what would he/she tell me?

_____

_____

_____

_____

_____

What do you think was the best part of the relationship with you for this person, something he/she will always carry with him/her?

_____

_____

_____

_____

_____

Reflection

What was it like for you to think about the mutual influence in this relationship? Does it have any effect on the way you see yourself?

_____

_____

_____

_____

_____

Conversation Exercise Week 5

> *Please get together with a friend or conversational partner. Talk about your reactions to the "Relational Identity" interview and about the idea of "Members of our Life Clubs."*

Readings for Week 5

Diener, E. & Biswas-Diener, R. (2008) Happiness Unlocking the Mysteries of Psychological Wealth. Malden MA: Blackwell. Chap. 4. Relationships

White, M. (2007). Maps of narrative practice. New York: W.W. Norton Chap. 3.Re-Membering Conversations.

Further Readings for Week 5

Gottman, J., & Silver, N. (1999). The Seven Principles for Making Marriage Work: A

Practical Guide from the Country's Foremost Relationship Expert. New York: Three Rivers Press.

References

Bartels, A., & Zeki, S. (2000). The Neural Basis of Romantic Love. Neuroreport 11, 3829-3834.

Csikszentmihalyi, M. (1997). Finding flow: the psychology of engagement with everyday life. . New York: Basic Books.

Diener, E., & Biswas-Diener, R. (2008). Happiness Unlocking the Mysteries of Psychological Wealth. Malden MA: Blackwell.

Fowler, J., & Christakis, N. (2008). Dynamic Spread of happiness in large social networks: longitudinal analysis over 20 years in the Framingham heart study. BMJ, 3337, a338+.

Fredrickson, B. (2009). Positivity: Groundbreaking Research Reveals How to Embrace the Hidden Strength of Positive Emotions, Overcome Negativity, and Thrive. . New York: Crown.

Freedman, J. &. (n.d.). Evanston Family Therapy Center. Retrieved September 19, 2010, from Characteristics of the Narrative World View: http://narrativetherapychicago.com/narrative worldview/narrative_worldview.htm

Gable, S. L., & Maisel, N. C. (2009). For Richer...in Good Times...and in Health: Positive Processes in Relationships. In S. Lopez, & C. Snyder, Oxford Handbook of Positive Psychology (pages. 445-462). New York: Oxford University Press.

Gable, S. L., Reis, H. T., Impett, E., & Asher, E. R. (2004). What do you do when things go right? The intrapersonal and interpersonal benefits of sharing positive events. Journal of Personality and Social Psychology 87, 228-245.

Gottman, J., & Silver, N. (1999). The Seven Principles for Making Marriage Work: A Practical Guide from the Country's Foremost Relationship Expert. New York: Three Rivers Press.

Harlow, H. F. (1958). The Nature of Love. American Psychologist, 13, 673-685.

Holt-Lunstad, J., Byron Smith, T., & Layton, B. (2010). Social relationships and mortality risk: A meta-analytic review. PLoS Medicine.

House, J., Landis, K., & Umberson, D. (1988). Social Relationships and Health. Science, 241(Jul 29), 540-545.

Kiecolt-Glaser, J., & Newton, T. (2001). Marriage and Health: His, Hers. Psychological Bulletin, 127, 472-503.

Peterson, C. (2006). A Primer in Positive Psychology. New York: Oxford University Press.

Peterson, C. (2008). Lecture Notes Positive Psychology Immersion Course. Mentor Coach.

Peterson, C. (s.f.). The Good Lfe. Recovered 11 April, 2009, from Psychology Today Blogs: /200806/other-people-matter-two-examples

Rath, T., & Harter., J. K. (2010). Well-being: the five essential elements. New York: Gallup Press.

Seligman, M. E. (2011). Flourish: a visionary new understanding of happiness and well-being. . New York, NY: Free Press.

Uchino, B., Cacioppo, J., & Kiecolt-Glaser, J. K. (1996). The Relationship between Social Support and Physiological Processes. Psychological Bulletin, 119(3), 488-531.

Vaillant, G. E. (2009). Obtained Positive Psychology News Daily: Vaillant, G. http://positivepsychologynews.com/news/George-vaillant/200907163163

White, M. (2007). Maps of narrative practice. New York: W.W. Norton.

White, M. &. (1990). Narrative Means to Therapeutic Ends (1 ed.). New York: W. W. Norton & Company.

Week 6   Purpose, Meaning and Achievements

Meaning and Achievement are the "M" and the "A" in PERMA [24], the acronym that summarizes the five elements of well-being, according to Martin Seligman (2011). In previous chapters we have examined the other elements of well-being, Positive Emotions, Engagement and Relationships, and you have reflected about how these contribute to your identity.

This week you will embark on an exploration of what contributes to a sense of meaning and purpose in your life: the values and commitments that guide your choices, your goals and dreams, and the steps you are taking to make them happen. The exercises for this last week of the course will also invite you to examine some of your greatest achievements, the ones that have been recognized by others and those that maybe only you know about. Finally, as in other weeks, I will encourage you to have conversations and generate dialogues about these topics with other people.

Meaning and Purpose in Your Life

Philosophers from time immemorial, ordinary people, therapists and research psychologists all agree that meaning in life is a key aspect of our existence. People want meaning and purpose in life (Seligman, 2011). The meaningful life, according to Seligman, consists in belonging to and serving something that you believe is bigger than yourself. He goes on to mention how societies build the institutions that allow us to achieve this. Political parties, the family, religions, and all sorts of organizations and groups are de- signed to help others and improve the world.

"Meaning permeates our lives," says Michael Steger, a specialist in the study of meaning from Colorado State University (2009, p. 679). He believes that meaning helps us interpret and organize our experiences, build a sense of our own worth, identify what matters to us and direct our energies effectively.

---
[24] Positivity, Engagement, Relationships, Meaning and Achievement.

In his overview of the research literature on meaning, Steger (2009) concludes that people who believe that their lives have meaning or purpose do better that those who don't. Among other things, they are happier, experience greater overall well-being and life satisfaction, have a greater sense of control over their lives, and are more engaged in their work. In other words, they have more of the "good things."

They also have fewer of the "not so good things." People with high levels of meaning have less negative affect, depression, and anxiety. They are less likely to be workaholic, to abuse drugs, or to have suicidal ideas. Research also indicates that people who have devoted their lives to a cause or ideal—something that transcends their immediate concerns—tend to have higher levels of meaning. On the other hand, people who are suffering from serious psychological distress, such as psychiatric patients and members of drug rehabilitation groups, tend to have lower levels of meaning. There is, however, some evidence that therapy may help these people rebuild meaning in their lives (ibid).

Having a purpose in life correlates with longevity, with life satisfaction, and with mental and physical health (Kashdan & McKnight, 2009). For example, McKnight & Kashdan (2009), report that people who volunteer have a mortality rate 60% lower than those who do not volunteer. Similarly, individuals who offer social support to others have half the death rate of people who do not offer or get social support. Even going beyond one's self in small ways, such as caring for a pet, is associated with longevity.

The concepts of meaning and purpose are intertwined. Before we see how they are defined by scholars, think about what each of these words means to you.

Psychologists who study meaning in life tend to emphasize two aspects of it: purpose and significance. Purpose generally refers to having certain important aims in our lives. Purpose is translated into behaviors: the actions we take and the goals we establish to get closer to these aims. Significance has to do with making sense of our lives, with the way we interpret our experiences so they become part of a coherent story.

I like the way Michael Steger defines meaning in life, incorporating these two aspects: "The extent to which people comprehend, make sense of, or see significance in their lives, accompanied by the degree to which they perceive themselves to have a purpose, mission or overarching goal in life" (2009, p.682).

Steger talks about the importance of meaning in our life narratives: "Life without meaning would be merely a string of events that fail to coalesce into a unified, coherent whole. A life without meaning is a life without a story, nothing to strive for, no sense of what might have been or what has been (Steger, M.2009, p.685)." Niemeyer & Mahoney (1995) also stress that our sense of meaning derives from our narratives and life stories.

Baumeister & Vohs (2005) propose that people look for meaningfulness in life to fulfill four basic needs:

- A need for purpose, to have goals and fulfillment from attaining them;
- A need for values, which give a sense of goodness to life and guide our actions;
- A sense of efficacy, to believe that we can make a difference;
- A sense of self-worth.

We will discuss purposes and goals later in the chapter. Let's take some time to think about the values that guide our actions. There are many ways to think about our values. To help you explore yours, we will use Shalom Schwartz's classification. He is a social psychologist who did a survey of over 60,000 people in 44 countries to see if there were certain common values that guided their lives. He found ten categories or kinds of values (Schwartz, 1994) and a certain structure or way in which these values tend to go together. They are:

1. **Power** - social status and prestige, ability to control others
2. **Achievement** - setting and achieving goals
3. **Hedonism** - seek pleasure and enjoyment
4. **Stimulation** - seeking excitement and thrills
5. **Self-direction** - prefer independence and freedom
6. **Universalism** - seek justice and tolerance
7. **Benevolence** - giving, helping others
8. **Tradition** - respect and preserve customs and world order
9. **Conformity** -obedience to rules and structures
10. **Security** - health and safety

Please take a few minutes to chart the role of each of these values in your life.

Exercise 6.1 Wheel of Values

A.   **The following diagram is based on Schwartz's classification of values.**

Look at each value and think about how important it is for you. To what extent does it guide your choices and decisions?

Fill out each "slice" of the graph, depending on its importance to you. If it is very important, fill the section. If it is not very important, just color a portion of it.

If there is a value that you think is not included, you can change the categories in the chart and write in your own as needed.

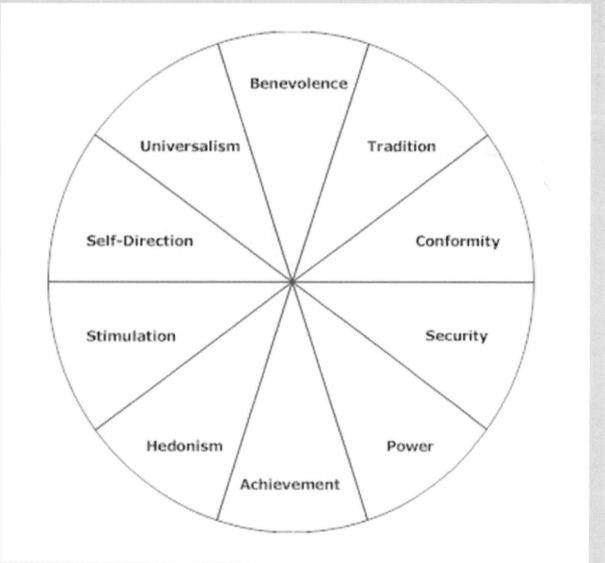

B. Pick one of the values from the wheel that is most important to you. Write it down please:

1. Why did you choose this value?

_____

_____

2. To what extent would you say it guides your decisions and the way you lead your life?

_____

_____

3. Can you think of a recent choice you made that was influenced by this value? How so?

_____

_____

_____

_____

4. How did you learn or acquire this value? Who was influential in your adoption of it?

_____

_____

5. What effects has upholding this value had on your life?_____

_____

_____

6. Are these positive or negative for you?_____

_____

_____

7. Is this value connected with one of your signature strengths? If yes, how?_____

_____

_____

Reflection

What is your reaction to this exercise?

_____

_____

_____

Our values, our sense of worth and efficacy, and our purpose and goals are all part of what makes life meaningful. For most people, there is rarely a single source of meaning; we tend to draw from several different sources (Baumeister & Vohs,2005). Studies about meaning often ask people "what gives meaning to your life?" and researchers then code and classify the participant's responses.

Exercise 6.2 Write a List
(Inspired by List Yourself, Segalove & Velick, 1996)

Please write a list of everything that comes to your mind when you are asked "What gives meaning to your life?" Don't think too much, just write what comes to your mind and try not to stop writing for 5 minutes.

_____

_____

_____

_____

_____

_____

_____

Robert Emmons (2003) has identified four frequent sources of meaning. They are: Work-Achievement; Intimacy-Relationships; Spirituality; and Transcendence-Generativity (dedicating our efforts to something beyond ourselves). What do you think? Do any of the items in your list fit within these categories? How relevant do these four areas seem to your own sense of meaningfulness in life?

Remember Eduardo, the man who built an Oriental City when he was a kid? I think that three of the four sources of meaning were very important to him: his relationship with his wife and children was wonderful, and central to his well-being. He always spoke of his spouse with great love and appreciation. Still, when he came to see me, his family relationships apparently were not enough to sustain a sense of well-being. When we spoke over several meetings, it became clear that work-achievement had been a very important source of meaning for him for years and he underestimated the toll that an early retirement would take on him. When he started to make his new occupation more challenging, work started to become meaningful for him again.

Transcendence and generativity were also important sources that Eduardo had put on hold. For many years he had been involved in community development. He organized a student's group in college and had worked with economically marginalized people in his home country. But then he had migrated and felt that as a foreigner he should not have any political activities. Interestingly, for him, community work was a form of "building" and we know how much he enjoyed building and repairing all kinds of things. This was a form of generativity for him. Unfortunately, I did not ask him about spirituality in his life. I wish I had; but it was clear that two important sources of meaning had been on the back burner for him, and he felt that he gained back his zest for life as he reactivated them.

Think about the four sources of meaning we have been discussing and please complete the following exercise:

Exercise 6.3 Interview with a Source of Meaning

(Inspired by Roth and Epston, 1996)

Warning: This exercise requires some imagination, but it is fun. Try it!

Please mark how important each factor on the right is for your sense of meaning in life.

	Not Important At All	Not Very Important	Somewhat Important	Very Important
Work-Achievement				
Intimacy-Relationships				
Spirituality				
Transcendence- Generativity				

Based on your answers, which one of these would you say is contributing more to your sense of meaning at this time in your life? (Please circle it)

- Work
- Intimacy
- Spirituality
- Transcendence

B.   Now imagine that source of meaning is a person or a character. We are going to interview it. For example, if you chose work, we will interview Work, or if you se lected spirituality, we will speak with Spirituality. You have to answer as if you were "Work," "Intimacy," "Spirituality," or "Transcendence," whichever one you just circled. Get into character, pretend you are Work or you are Spirituality, or Transcendence, or Intimacy. Imagine I am the interviewer and answer the questions as if you were that character [25]. Write your actual name (Nancy, George) where it says "your name." Ready?

1.   Hello_____(Work, Intimacy, Spirituality or Transcendence. Write which one you are for this interview.) Thank you for being willing to talk with me.

2.   Were you surprised to learn that you play such an important role in_____'s (your name) life?

_____

3.   Why are you/are you not surprised?

_____

_____

4.   Can you tell me a little about your relationship with_____(your name)? How did you two meet?

_____

_____

_____

_____

5.   How long ago?

_____

_____

6.   Did anyone introduce you?

_____

_____

[25] If you can do this with a friend, take turns interviewing each other. Do the whole interview before switching places. Remember you have to speak as if you were work, or transcendence, or intimacy or spirituality. Have fun with it

7.   **What kinds of things do you do together?**

_____

_____

_____

_____

8.   **What would you say is your main contribution to_____(your name) ´s life?**

_____

_____

9.   **How does_____(your name) nurture you?**

_____

_____

10.   **Are there ways_____(your name) may sometimes neglect you?**

_____

_____

11.   **Any ideas for_____(your name) about how to help you thrive?**

_____

_____

_____

12.   **What are your hopes for_____(your name) in the future?**

_____

_____

_____

13.   **Anything else you would like us to know about you?**

_____

_____

_____

Thank you!

Reflections

What did this exercise make you think and feel?

_____

_____

_____

_____

I know that the exercise may have seemed a little weird, but I hope it helped you think some more about the sources of meaning in your life. Did it remind you of the externalization exercise that we did in Chapter 3? It's based on the same idea. If we think of meaning as something that we either have or don't have inside of us, our ideas may be limited. But if we think of meaning as something that exists in our lives, something we relate to and can nurture or neglect, we can come up with more possibilities about how to increase its presence and its positive impact in our lives [26].

---

[26] In different types of studies about meaning, "relationships" usually comes as the source of meaning top for many people. Was this the case for you? (There is no right answer; I was just curious.)

Purpose

As we mentioned earlier, purpose in life generally refers to something more tangible than meaning. Our purposes are aligned with specific aims and goals. Have you seen how some companies have framed prints of their mission statements in their offices? We could think of our life purpose as our mission, what we want to accomplish while we are on this planet, the small or big difference that we want our lives to make.

Kashdan and McKnight define purpose as "a central, self-organized life aim that organizes and stimulates goals, manages behaviors and provides a sense of meaning" (2009, p.242). For these authors, purpose is a kind of inner compass that helps us direct our behavior. Using a nice analogy, they say that our purpose can be like a compass. Using a compass is optional, so is following our purpose. But if we do, it provides us with a sense of meaning because it helps us create and attain goals in our lives. "Purpose is woven into a person's identity and behavior (p.242)."

Kashdan and McKnight (2009) point out that we can have multiple purposes. This can be beneficial because if we are focused exclusively on one project or goal and it does not work out, it can be very dismaying. However, if we have too many purposes, they tend to dilute each other and we need to choose where to devote our energy and effort.

Have you ever thought about your purpose(s) in life? If you were a company and had your purpose or mission printed, framed and displayed on a wall, what would it say? I think many of us have an intuitive sense of our purpose, but we don't always articulate it.

As Dr. Seligman mentions (2011), humanity has built many institutions that help us feel we are part of something bigger than us. Belonging to these institutions can help us live more meaningful lives. The groups or organizations that you are or have been a part of may hold clues about your purpose(s) in life. The places and people with whom you felt you were a good "fit," where you engaged in activities that brought you satisfaction and inspiration, can tell you much about your purposes. These can include a school, a music band, a church or religious organization, a bird watching club, an emergency medical clinic.

For example, when I think of important institutions and organizations in my life (in addition to my family), the first things that come to my mind are my school (which I attended from preschool through high-school), the University of Chicago, where I went to graduate school, and the family therapy institutes where I trained, as well as the professional organizations, communities of collaborative and narrative practitioners and positive psychologists of which I am a member.

I think these give me some hints about the importance of learning and academics in my life, and about my vocation of service to others. And what do I do at work? I spend about 50% of my time teaching in universities and 50% working with clients trying to help them flourish and live a full life.

Exercise 6.4 Hints of Purpose: Important Groups and Institutions in Your Life

Think of the groups or organizations that you are or have been a part of, which have had a positive impact in your life. Make a list of them in the first column and briefly describe what they were devoted to in the next.

Institution, Group, Club or Organization	What It Does
_____	_____
_____	_____
_____	_____
_____	_____
_____	_____

Reflection

What are you thinking? What stood out for you? Did you see any commonalities or common threads? Did you remember one organization that was particularly important to you?

_____

_____

_____

There are many ways to explore and define our life purpose. Caroline Miller and Michael Frisch are specialists in positive psychology. They wrote one of my favorite books, Creating your Best Life (Miller & Frisch, 2009), and in it there is a chapter on mission statements. Miller & Frisch offer the six following steps as guidelines to create an individual mission statement:

1. *Ask yourself what your most cherished values are.*

2. *Ask yourself how you want others, including your children, to remember you after you're gone.*

3. *Ask yourself what words or phrases inspire your most from history, current events, politics, humanism, or religious work. Peruse a quote book or inter net site to get ideas if you need them.*

4. *Look at the mission statement of successful companies on their websites, delivery trucks, or letterhead and ask yourself if those phrases elicit a feeling in you that matches what the product actually delivers.*

5. *Be sure that your final mission statement is compelling, action oriented, inspirational, simple and easy to understand. It should at once state your goals while eliciting your best self and most authentic behavior.*

6. *Don't worry if you do not get it right the first time. Keep trying until you feel the fit (Miller & Frisch, 2009, pp. 150-151).*

Kashdan and McKnight stress that, "purpose is woven into a person's identity and behavior (p.242)." It is one axis around which we organize the stories of our lives and the sense of who we are. In narrative work, when a person feels limited by certain description of his or her life and we want to help this person explore and develop alternative stories, we embark on a joint exploration of this person's longings, hopes and dreams, values, commitments and purposes (White, 2004). This often changes the negative conclusions that people may have about their identity.

Here is an exercise that invites you to think about your values, dreams as they relate to your work:

Exercise 6.5 Values, Dreams and Inspiration
(Inspired by Harlene Anderson's and Michael White's ideas)

Think about the time in your life when you decided that you wanted to be a _____ _____(write your occupation or profession) or to take your current job as a_____(write the name of your work)

How did you come to that decision?_____
_____
_____

What values, intentions and dreams guided your decision? _____
_____
_____

Why were these important to you?_____
_____
_____

What do you think this says about you as a person?_____
_____
_____

Are these values, intentions and dreams still important at this time? If they have changed, which would you say are important to you now?_____
_____
_____

How much can you keep these values, hopes and dreams present in your everyday work? _____
_____

Is there something that makes it difficult to keep them present?_____
_____
_____

What makes it easier to keep them alive in your work?_____
_____
_____

If there was one thing you could do to increase or renew the presence of these values, intentions and dreams in your daily work, what would it be?_____
_____
_____

What impact could this have on your work?_____
_____
_____

If you could build your "dream team," a group of people who could help you be the way you want to be professionally, who would be the members of that team?_____
_____
_____

Reflection

What is your inner dialogue after doing this exercise? What are you thinking and feeling?_____

_____

_____

Michael White believed that when we "richly describe" our values, dreams, sources of inspiration and hopes, exploring them in detail in our conversations, we can generate more positive identity conclusions. I know that "identity conclusions" may sound like an awkward phrase, but it is used intentionally to highlight that our identity is not a monolith that exists inside of us. It is a construction; it is dynamic. We reach conclusions about who we are based on our experiences and our interactions with other people and these conclusions are subject to revisions and development. These different conclusions about themselves can encourage people to take steps so their actions and relationships will be more aligned with their purposes in life.

Imagine that I ask you, as many college applications do, to write your autobiography. This may be a daunting task. (It was for me in those university applications.) How does one start, how to organize many experiences in a way that makes sense?

Now imagine you get a little help. You are given some of the chapter headings. They include:

- Your longings, hopes and dreams [27]
- Your values
- Your commitments
- Your purposes
- The knowledge you have about life and the actions you take in terms of these values, hopes and dreams.

---

[27] Not what you dream at night, but your "dreams" as in what you would most like for yourself and others.

It would be a little easier to write about yourself this way, wouldn't it? These categories help us organize our identity.

You have already examined some of your most important values and the sources of meaning in your life, as well as the organizations that may have shaped, or are sustaining your sense of purpose.

Now imagine that somebody in the future is going to write your biography. Your name would be the title and you have to choose the subtitle, a phrase or a couple of words that would summarize your life's purpose. For example, there is The Story of Walt Disney: Maker of Magical Worlds (Selden, 2009), Marie Curie: The Woman Who Changed the Course of Science

Exercise 6.6 Title of Your Biography

(Steele, 2008), or Always the Poor, Mother Teresa: Her Life and Message. (González-Balado, 1980).

Write the name of your biography on the book cover.

In her book, Creating Your Best Life: The Ultimate Life List Guide (Miller & Frisch, 2009, p. 249), Caroline Miller has an exercise called "Portrait of your Life," which helps you explore in more detail how you would like to be remembered.

Goals

Are goals different than purposes? McKnight and Kashdan (2009) explain that goals are more specific than purpose. Purpose is a larger construct, maybe more abstract, that motivates people to have goals and it organizes those goals. For example, if your purpose is to save Earth's coral reefs, you need to establish concrete goals to achieve this.

For example, you might set goals to identify the most vulnerable reefs in the world, decide which are the ones where you can have a more immediate impact, contact the Cousteau Foundation to apply for research grant, write the Secretary of the Environment in your country, assemble a group of volunteers to visit elementary schools and educate children about marine environments, establish an alliance with the World Scuba Diving Association to limit dives in certain reefs, and so on. Goals are the practical steps that can lead you to fulfill your purpose.

Goal setting and attainment is one of the most exciting areas studied by positive psychology because they are important components of well-being. There are researchers who study how people establish goals and what helps them reach these goals. Among them are Edwin Locke and Gary Latham, from the University of Maryland and the University of Toronto, respectively. Their studies (Locke & Latham, 1990) show that it is more likely we will reach a goal if:

1. **The Goal is Challenging.** If we have the skill and knowledge needed for the task, it is more likely that we will reach a difficult goal than an easy one. For example, if we like to run, we can set the goal of running a 10 k race in the Spring instead of running in a 5 k competition.

2. **The Goal is Specific.** It is important to have a clear and concrete definition of what we want to achieve, in observable and measurable terms. To say that you will "do your best" is not specific. Instead, if you say "I will increase my sales 10%," or "I will exercise at the gym four times a week, an hour each time," you will have set clear and objective goals.

3. **We get feedback.** We spoke about the importance of feedback in the chapter about engagement and flow. Remember how we are more likely to

have a flow experience if the activity offers us feedback? This is relevant for goals too, as Locke and Latham have found. In order to gauge our progress towards a goal, we need to know how we are doing, what our partial results are along the way. For example, if you are training for the 10 k race, you will probably start doing shorter runs, timing them and assessing how tired you feel after each one. When you see that you can handle 5 k without collapsing, you may try 6 k the next weekend. If you are trying to lose weight, it is important to step on the scale periodically. And students know that it is better to have several partial evaluations in a class than to have their grade based on one final exam.

4. **<u>Commitment is fundamental.</u>** If we want to achieve a goal, we need to be committed to it. Generally, we are more likely to only commit to goals that are important to us (intrinsic), not just to other people.

Locke and Latham emphasize that there are no shortcuts to achieve goals; they require hard work. Our values and goals motivate us and lead us to action. Lock also has found that fear is one of the main obstacles to goal attainment: fear of changing, fear of failure, fear of making mistakes. It is important not to let these fears get in our way of our striving for what we value (Locke & Latham, 1990; Miller & Frisch, 2009). Similarly, Angela Duckworth and Martin Seligman have studied what distinguishes high achieving people from others with similar talents but fewer achievements. They found the key was "grit," a combination of being tenacious, hardworking, passionate and not giving up when things are difficult (Miller & Frisch, 2009; Duckworth & Seligman, 2005).

Exercise 6.7 Your "Bucket List" (from Caroline Miller)

Go to Caroline Miller's website (http://carolinemillercoaching.com/worksheets.html) and do the "One Hundred Things to Do Before I Die" exercise.

Reflection

What was it like for you to think of 100 goals?_____

_____

_____

Did anything surprise you?_____

_____

_____

Did something move you?_____

_____

_____

Do you see patterns or connections between your goals and some of your values or purposes?____

_____

_____

Miller & Frisch (2009), state that people have a higher chance of achieving a goal if they write it rather than if they just think or talk about it. There is also evidence that there is a greater chance of achieving a goal if we are accountable to someone, for example, if we commit to exercising with a buddy instead of doing it on our own. In their book, Creating your Best Life (2008), Miller & Frisch invite us to write down our goals and ask ourselves these questions:

- *Is this goal specific and measurable?*
- *Is it challenging?*
- *Is it connected to a value that it important for me?*
- *What steps are necessary to achieve this goal?*
- *What obstacles may I face and how will I overcome them?*
- *How can I increase my commitment and motivation?*
- *How will I know I am making progress? What are the intermediate goals?*
- *Whom will I be accountable to? Who is part of my team to achieve this goal?*

(Miller & Frisch, 2009, pp. 238-239)

Another important factor in goal attainment is self-determination. Kashdan and McKnight point out that there are several studies that show that people make more progress towards their goals and show greater psychological health and flexibility when their actions are self-determined (self-selected and congruent with a person´s preferences and values) (Kashdan & McKnight, 2009). Deci and Ryan have found that self-determined goals promote autonomy, foster a sense of competence and help us relate and connect with others (Deci & Ryan, 2000).

Accomplishment

Dr. Martin Seligman recently added "Accomplishment" to his theory of well-being. Some years ago, in Authentic Happiness (2002) he proposed that there were three pillars of happiness: the pleasant life (experiencing pleasure and positive emotions), the engaged life (having flow experiences and using our personal strengths), and the meaningful life (a sense of transcendence or being connected to something larger than our- selves). He later added "Relationships" as another key for a full life. In his most recent book, Flourish (2011), Seligman recounts how, thanks to the questions posed to him by his MAPP [28] student Senia Maymin, he became convinced that people strive for accomplishment and achievement, sometimes independently of whether they bring pleasure or meaning to their lives. But most of the time, achievement, like the other elements of well-being, is intertwined with the other factors (Seligman, 2011).

For example, a soccer player who wants to win the World Cup will probably experience a lot of engagement during his practices and while playing in the championship. He may develop very important relationships with his teammates and may even decide to donate part of the money he makes from endorsements to charity. But competency (mastering an activity, like scoring goals or kicking across the field) is often an important motivation in itself.

One of the most interesting research findings about achievement is that effort we put into accomplishing something, the sheer amount of time we devote to achieving a task

[28] Master's in Applied Positive Psychology

or to develop a skill, is perhaps the most important predictor of success. Persevering and dedicating time and effort are decisions that depend on our will, our self-control and grit. We can do something about them, they are malleable (Seligman,2011).

Here is an exercise to explore some of your most important achievements.

Exercise 6.8 Your Stories of Achievement

(Adapted from "The 7 Stories Exercise" by Kate Wendleton, 1999)

Think of the times in your life when you have felt a great sense of accomplishment. Times when you did something well and felt you had achieved something important for you. They can be things that other people considered achievements, too, or experiences that only you knew represented an accomplishment. Scan all areas of your life: school, work, family, community. You can go back to your childhood, your teens, all the way up to the present. It is important to describe them in specific terms. For example, "my senior year in high school" is too vague. "Organizing the art fair in my senior year of high school" is more precise. "My marriage" would also be too broad, but "working two shifts for three years while my spouse went to graduate school" gives a more specific account. This exercise is usually done over a few days. You can jot things down (or record them) as you remember.

A.   **Write down at least ten of these success experiences.**

1. _____
2. _____
3. _____
4. _____
5. _____
6. _____
7. _____
8. _____
9. _____
10. _____

B.   Now choose five of these experiences. Describe them in as much detail as you can. What exactly did you do? How did you prepare for this? What strengths and skills did this require on your part? How much effort did you put into it? Was it related to your values? Did it fit with your hopes and purposes? Why was this an important accomplishment for you?

1. _____

_____

_____

_____

_____

_____

_____

_____

2. _____

_____

_____

_____

_____

_____

_____

_____

_____

3. _____

_____

_____

_____

_____

_____

_____

_____

_____

4. _____

_____

_____

_____

_____

_____

_____

5. _____

_____

_____

_____

_____

_____

_____

Reflection

What was the process of remembering and describing important accomplishments like for you?_____

_____

_____

_____

_____

This brings us to the last section of our workbook: pride and acknowledgment. The word "proud" can evoke mixed reactions. We can use it to refer to someone who will not accept that she has made a mistake, or who cannot forgive. But "proud" can also describe how we feel when we have reached a goal that required a lot of effort. We can also feel proud of other people when we see them accomplishing their dreams or demonstrating their strengths.

Pride is actually one of the positive emotions that Barbara Fredrickson studied (2009) and she found that it contributes to our well-being, especially if it is combined with a dose of humility. We feel proud when we feel responsible for something good, when we can recognize the skills and efforts that were needed to accomplish what we did. Fredrickson says that feeling pride can help us expand our horizons and imagine what else we could do. "Nothing succeeds like success," and if we have succeeded at something, we are motivated to face even bigger challenges. Studies show that when people feel pride, they don't give up easily and they persist in the face of challenges (op.cit.).

We are approaching the end of our six weeks together. I would like to finish with an exercise in acknowledgement. In narrative practices, it is important to recognize "alternative stories" to make them stronger, and to write documents that bear witness to important developments in a person's life (White & Epston, 1990).

 Some time ago, a woman named Olga came to see me for consultation. (Tarragona M. , 2003). We worked with a team. I would interview her, and at the end of each meeting the members of the team would share their reflections about our conversation. At the end of the process, after eight sessions, we gave Olga a diploma. On it, each of us wrote what we thought she had demonstrated in our time together. People mentioned her intelligence, sense of humor, perseverance, love for her children, and capacity to adapt. One wrote "for being like the Phoenix Bird," because she had overcome serious tragedies in her life. Six months later, a colleague of mine who was doing a research project interviewed Olga about her experience. She told us that sometimes she would take her diploma and re-read it. "Why?" my colleague asked. "Because it reminds me about who I am," she said.

As you read this book and did the exercises, what have you learned, or remembered, about who you are? What aspects of your identity would you like to be reminded of once in a while?

Take some time to review all the work you have done in the past six weeks. What did you enjoy the most? What made you think the most? Do you feel you have enriched or "thickened" the descriptions of yourself? Do you have any new ideas about your preferred self?

Exercise 6.9 Your Diploma

Please fill in this diploma. Give it to yourself in recognition of some of your skills, strengths, values and dreams.

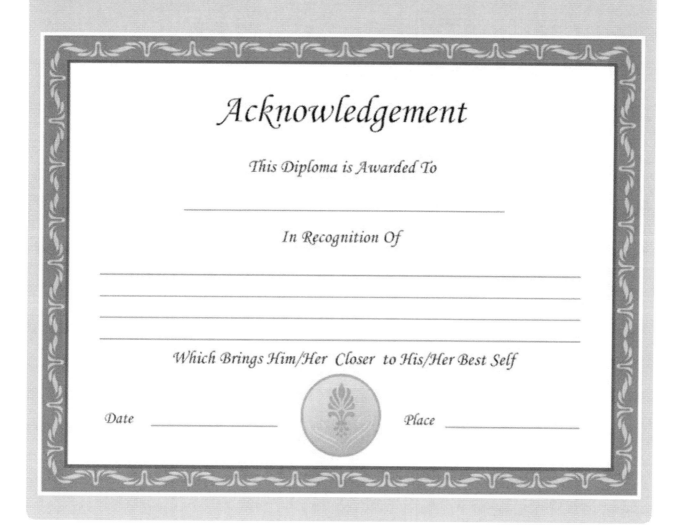

Keep this diploma, and all of the exercises you have done, to remind you of the best versions of yourself.

Thanks for all your work and my best wishes for you!

Conversation Exercise Week 6

Please get together with a friend or conversational partner. Talk about your experience of working on this workbook for six weeks. What stood out for you? What has been interesting? Fun? Would you say you have enriched the way you see yourself? Are you a little closer to your preferred identities?

Readings for Week 6

Miller, C. A., & Frisch, M. B. (2009). Creating your best life: the ultimate life list guide. New York: Sterling.

Seligman, M. E. (2011). Flourish: a visionary new understanding of happiness and well-being. New York, NY: Free Press. Chap. 6

Further Readings for Week 6

Kashdan, T., & McKnight, P. (2009). Origins of purpose in life: Refining our understanding of a life well lived. Psychological Topics, 18, [Special Issue on Positive Psychology], 303-316.

Steger, M. (2009). Meaning in Life. In S. Lopez, & C. Snyder, Oxford Handbook of

Positive Psychology, Second Edition (pp. 679-687). New York: Oxford University Press.

References

Baumeister, R., & Vohs, K. (2005). The Pursuit of Meaningfulness in Life. In C. Snyder, & S. J. Lopez, Handbook of Positive Psychology (pp. 608-618). New York: Oxford University Press.

Deci, E. I., & Ryan, R. M. (2000). Self-Determination Theory and the Facilitation of Intrinsic Motivation, Social Development and Well-being. American Psychologist.

Duckworth, A., & Seligman, M. (2005). Self-Discipline Outdoes IQ in Predicting Academic Performance of Adolescents. Psychological Science, 16, 939-944.

Emmons, R. (2003). Personal goals, life meaning, and virtue: Wellsprings of a positive life. In C. K. (Ed.), Flourishing; The positive person and the good life. (pp. 105-128). Washington, DC: American Psychological Association.

Fredrickson, B. (2009). Positivity: Groundbreaking Research Reveals How to Embrace the Hidden Strength of Positive Emotions, Overcome Negativity, and Thrive. New York: Crown.

Kashdan, T., & McKnight, P. (2009). Origins of purpose in life: Refining our understanding of a life well lived. Psychological Topics, 18, [Special Issue on Positive Psychology], 303-316.

Locke, E., & Latham, G. (1990). A Theory of Goal Setting and Task Performance. Englewood Cliffs, NJ: Prentice Hall.

Miller, C. A., & Frisch, M. B. (2009). Creating your best life: the ultimate life list guide. New York: Sterling.

Niemeyer, R., & Mahoney, J. (1995). Constructivism in Psychology. Washington, DC: APA.

Roth, S., & Epston, D. (1996). Consulting the Problem about the Problematic Relationship: An Exercise for Experiencing a Relationship with an Externalized Problem. In M. Hoyt, Constructive Therapies vol. II, New York: Guilford.

Schwartz, S. (1994). Schwartz, S. H. (1994), Are There Universal Aspects in the Structure and Contents of Human Values? Journal of Social Issues, 50, 19–45.

Seligman, M. E. (2002). Authentic happiness: using the new positive psychology to realize your potential for lasting fulfillment. New York: Free Press.

Seligman, M. E. (2011). Flourish: a visionary new understanding of happiness and well-being. New York, NY: Free Press.

Steger, M. (2009). Meaning in Life. In S. Lopez, & C. Snyder, Oxford Handbook of Positive Psychology, Second Edition (pp. 679-687). New York: Oxford University Press.

Wendleton, K. (1999). Building a Great Resume. New York: Career Press.

White, M. (2004). Narrative Practice and Exotic Lives: Resurrecting diversity in everyday life. Adelaide, South Australia: Dulwich Centre Publications.

White, M., & Epston, D. (1990). Narrative Means to Therapeutic Ends (1 ed.). New York: W. W. Norton & Company.

Made in the USA
Lexington, KY
18 June 2019